EATING
with the
VICTORIANS

EATING
with the
VICTORIANS

Edited by C. Anne Wilson

Foreword by Tom Jaine

SUTTON PUBLISHING

This book was first published in 1994 under the title
Luncheon, Nuncheon and other Meals by
Sutton Publishing Limited · Phoenix Mill
Thrupp · Stroud · Gloucestershire · GL5 2BU

This paperback edition first published in 2004

British Library Cataloguing in Publication Data
A catalogue record for this book is available from the
British Library

ISBN 0 7509 3551 0

Typeset in 12/14pt Photina.
Typesetting and origination by
Sutton Publishing Limited.
Printed and bound in Great Britain by
J.H. Haynes & Co. Ltd, Sparkford.

CONTENTS

Acknowledgements

All illustrations not separately acknowledged in their captions have been reproduced from books in the Brotherton Library, University of Leeds, and the editor and contributors would like to express their gratitude to the University Librarian for granting permission for the reproductions to appear in this book. The editor would like to thank everyone who has given help towards the preparation of the book, and especially the following: Miss F. Dimond, Curator, Photograph Collection, Royal Archives, Windsor; Mrs B. Holden of the Centre for Rural Studies, University of Reading; Mrs S. Ayres, Administrator, Linley Sambourne House, London; Ms D. Kidd of the Scottish Ethnological Archive, Royal Museum of Scotland, Edinburgh; and Mrs A. Farr and Mr C. Sheppard of the Brotherton Library, University of Leeds.

FOREWORD

TOM JAINE

Breakfast, lunch, tea and dinner: the succession seems immutable, the context written in stone. Yet, faced with the chapters in this book, the reader is likely to be as unhinged as was the intrepid Edwardian traveller in the Balkans, Edith Durham. 'The Albanians', she discovered, 'have a custom, cruel to those that are not to the manner born. No matter what is the time of year, they eat rather before midday and again one hour after sunset, or even later.' To cap it all, the hour of sunset was termed twelve o'clock, winter and summer. Hence mealtimes, just as the clock, were relative. So, you might argue, were they in Britain, where dinner moved from nine o'clock in the morning to nine at night in the course of five centuries; yet here it was the rhythm of the working day that supplied the motive force, rather than the passage of the sun.

It soon becomes plain that mere nourishment has less influence on the form and timing of meal-taking than would at first seem likely. Social rank, the need for conspicuous display, the mechanics of social intercourse: all appear more significant factors. Hence, even today, if a businessman needs to conduct his affairs through the medium of breakfast or lunch meetings, those meals will assume greater importance in his life than ever they would have done were he a farm labourer. Yet he has less nutritional requirement than most of his fellow citizens, but restaurants in cities thrive at lunchtime, while those in the country are closed.

A similar dynamic is suggested for the development of lunch. Victorian ladies had longer and lazier days than their Georgian forebears; they needed to fill the hours; they invented lunch.

It comes, therefore, as less of a surprise that meals and mealtimes underwent such radical change in the Victorian era. It was a time of acute shifts in society, at all levels; when there was not just upward or downward mobility — new people stepping into old habits — but a reconstruction of the whole ladder of improvement. Add to this the effects of technical and economic change on people's everyday lives — the journey to work, wage-slavery, new household equipment, new forms of information — and it becomes apparent that few corners of life would be unaffected.

Victorian novelists, for instance Surtees or Trollope, lay bare the extreme social anxiety surrounding meals and mealtimes. It was not just what time they were, though the hour might show exactly a person's rank or aspirations, but also their form. Were the courses at dinner served *à l'Anglaise* or *à la Russe?* Was lunch some light collation or a full-blown meal? The fact that there were two variables — time *and* content — meant that the interpretations of a person's eating habits were infinite in number. He or she might have taste, but be of a social condition that imposed an early dinner, and so on. Then, there are regional variations, north and south, town and country. It all makes a rich compost, fit for much speculation.

'The legitimate objects of dinner are to refresh the body, please the palate, and to raise the social humour to the highest point', commented the gastronome Thomas Walker. 'But these objects', he continued, 'so far from being studied, in general, are not even thought of, and display and adherence to fashion are their meagre substitutes.' This book hastens understanding of that contradiction.

INTRODUCTION

MEAL PATTERNS AND FOOD SUPPLY IN VICTORIAN BRITAIN

C. ANNE WILSON

If we could be transported back more than two hundred years to spend a day in the eighteenth century, one of the surprises for most people would be the difference in the timing and structure of meals. Even when Queen Victoria came to the throne in 1837, luncheon had only recently become established as a proper meal, and many professional men refused to accept it because it cut into their working hours across the middle of the day. The upper and middle classes dined at 5.00 p.m. in the 1830s, while dinner for servants, artisans and less fashionable folk continued to take place around one or two o'clock, as it had done for the previous two centuries.

The drinking of tea some two hours after dinner had become customary during the later eighteenth century when the fashionable hour for dining was

3.00 or 4.00 p.m.; and in Scotland and northern England this form of refreshment was beginning in the 1820s and '30s to expand into a full-scale late afternoon or early evening meal, with the addition of cakes, pastry and in due course cold meats as well. But the tea meal did not even win a mention in the 1861 first edition of Isabella Beeton's *The Book of Household Management*, and was not added until the enlarged edition of 1880.

Today our timetable for meals still reflects patterns established during the nineteenth century, and the story of those Victorian meals is set out in the chapters of this book, which originated at the meeting of the Leeds Symposium on Food History held in April 1992 on the theme of 'Nineteenth-century Meals and Mealtimes'. The speakers there set a context for each meal through the day, outlining its development during earlier centuries before moving on to the Victorian meal, as recorded in contemporary literature and contemporary cookery books, which formed the core of their talks. The only exception was a talk on the important role of Victorian cookery and household books in standardizing patterns for the meals.

This last subject provides a central chapter in our book. The knowledge spread by the cookery literature of the later nineteenth century extended well beyond recipes into the realm of garnishes, table decoration and how to serve your meal to guests. This sort of information was sought eagerly by an ever-expanding middle class of families who were upwardly mobile in their social lives, and were anxious to entertain their friends and acquaintances in the correct manner. The obsession with correctness increased as Queen Victoria's reign progressed, calling forth new books and new editions of old ones. Mrs Beeton's *The Book of Household Management* (1861) and J.H. Walsh's *A Manual of Domestic Economy* (1859) had to be amplified in new editions from the late 1870s onwards to include much fuller advice on how to serve meals *à la Russe*, for that had now become the fashionable way to dine. Some of the social pitfalls can be seen in contemporary cartoons published in *Punch*.

Only a few cookery books were concerned with the cookery of the 'deserving' poor. At their end of the social scale the problem was not so much the manner of cooking and serving food as how to obtain enough of it in the first place. The 'hungry forties' were the most memorable period of near starvation, but there were others. Edward Smith's survey of the weekly expenditure of the families of several hundred agricultural labourers and poorly paid industrial workers showed that 'the diet of these numerically large classes was as bad in 1863 as it had been at any time earlier in the century.'[1]

Poor families tended to buy their limited range of foodstuffs in very small amounts at a time, and indeed they consumed relatively little bacon, cheese, milk and butter in addition to their mainstay of bread and, where available, potatoes. Furthermore, much of the food bought by the poor was heavily adulterated. This situation improved only very slowly after it was given a good deal of publicity during the 1850s through the reports in the *Lancet* by Arthur Hassall, and through the more popular books and newspaper and magazine articles based on the information he had supplied. Nevertheless, legislation passed in 1860 allowed for the appointment of public analysts on a voluntary, not a mandatory, basis; and it was not until 1872 that further legislation led to increased inspection of food offered for sale, and to a large number of convictions for its adulteration. Finally the Sale of Food and Drugs Act 1875 brought about a really significant improvement in the purity of food.[2]

Another improvement which took place during Queen Victoria's reign was that increasing numbers of houses were equipped with cast-iron kitchen ranges which included ovens and water heaters. Before the end of the century gas ovens were available. In the earlier decades town-dwellers with small houses and limited cooking facilities had carried their Sunday joints and Christmas fowls and puddings to the nearest bakery to be cooked in the baker's ovens. By the end of the century this custom had all but died out.

The choice of foodstuffs increased as more produce was brought back from the territories within Britain's empire, and in the later decades of the reign the cost of some of the more basic foods fell. Distribution of food within Britain became easier as the railway system grew. From the 1870s onwards imported American wheat meant cheaper bread. At the same time canned meat from Australia and America began to arrive in increasing quantities, and although much of it was coarse and not very appetizing (unless well seasoned in stews and pies), it did allow people to eat beef and mutton even if they could not afford to buy fresh home-killed meat. From 1880 onwards frozen meat was brought from Australia and Argentina in ships with refrigerated holds, and that too sold at a lower price than fresh meat. Fish supplies became more plentiful and cheaper when steam trawlers brought back cod and other fish packed in ice, and these were rapidly distributed by rail to inland towns. During the last twenty years of Queen Victoria's reign the cod became the mainstay of the newly emerging fried fish and chip shops in the industrial towns.

Through those two decades food prices in general fell in relation to wages, and more people could enjoy the occasional treat of canned fruits from warmer climates, imported mainly from Australia and the New World. China tea, which had become a staple of diet for all classes (the poor brewing their tea from cheap blends heavily adulterated with old, reused tea leaves, leaves from native British trees, and often dangerous chemical substances, too), was gradually supplanted from 1870 onwards by far less expensive teas from India and Ceylon.[3]

By the last years of the Victorian era the timing of meals had fallen into a pattern which is still widely followed today. Sir Henry Thompson described in *Food and Feeding* (8th edition, 1894, p. 142) two coexisting systems: that of Londoners and

of the numerous English families throughout the country whose habits are formed from partial residence in town, or by more or less intimate acquaintance with town life [whose system] is that of three meals daily. In general terms the breakfast takes place between eight and ten, the lunch about two, the dinner from seven to half past eight or even later.

What I have termed the provincial system consists of a substantial breakfast at eight or nine, a dinner at one or two, a light tea about five, and a supper at nine or ten. It is this which is popular throughout our provincial districts, and also among middle-class society of our northern districts throughout both town and country.

Apart from the fact that he gives rather less prominence to high tea than many families would today, his systems are very close to ours. But today a new generation has already emerged which favours the browsing or snack culture. It would be interesting to know whether this approach will eventually drive out the structured meal patterns we have inherited from the Victorians.

But now, on to the meals themselves. We hope you will find them to your taste.

ONE

FIRST THINGS FIRST: THE GREAT BRITISH BREAKFAST

EILEEN WHITE

It is generally acknowledged that the British breakfast is one of our chief assets. Any visitor to this country expects to start the day with bacon, eggs and sausages, perhaps accompanied by tomatoes or mushrooms, and followed by toast and marmalade. The ideal setting is seen as the Victorian or Edwardian country house, and it is to the Victorian era that we must look for the full development of this meal, although it had taken several hundred years to reach perfection. But does our conception of the traditional fare represent the true glory of the Victorian breakfast?

THE PRE-VICTORIAN BREAKFAST

In looking at the early development of this meal, the most striking fact is that many writers tried to make us believe it did not exist, while others gave glimpses of better things. Its importance relates to the times of other meals in the day, the main dinner and smaller supper. Medieval household ordinances often prescribe dinner in summer at ten o'clock in the morning, with supper at five in the evening; in winter the times would be nine o'clock and four o'clock. Henry VIII kept similar hours in 1526, when the court was in residence; at other times his household would eat at eleven o'clock and six o'clock. However, masters and servants did not have to wait until dinner before eating: Edward IV had bread, a portion of unspecified food from the kitchen and half a gallon of ale for his breakfast in 1472, and Henry VIII's courtiers had bread and a gallon of ale allocated in the mornings, according to regulations of 1526. In 1543 Queen Katherine Parr's maids had a chine of beef daily for their breakfast.[1] Other noble households had similar allocations, and in 1512 the Earl of Northumberland's family had bread, beer, wine, salt fish, herring or sprats on fast days, and a chine of mutton or beef, or a chicken, on meat days.[2]

Andrew Boorde in 1542 described a healthy regime that omitted breakfast, stating: 'Two meals a day is suffycent for a rest man and a labourer may eate three tymes a day; & he that doth eate ofter, lyueth a beestly lyfe'; yet elsewhere he admits that 'poched egges be best at nyght, & newe reare rosted egges be good in the mornynge, so be it they be tyred with a lyttell salt and suger' — by which he probably meant eggs either cooked on a baker's peel, or grilled by having a hot salamander held over them; they should not be fried, for 'fryed egges be nought'.[3]

Two meals a day continued to be seen as the ideal, but William Harrison in 1587 appreciated that living so far north, Englishmen needed more nourishment. He was, however, pleased to see that 'breakfasts in the forenoon' and other odd repasts were no longer used, and that all but younger people were contented with dinner and supper only.[4] Through the sixteenth century, the time of dinner gradually moved to noon, an example set by the merchants according to Harrison, while the court and the universities kept to the earlier hour. An evocative description of a typical day by Nicholas Breton in 1626 shows the variety of mealtimes across the social spectrum, starting with the servants' pot of porridge on the fire by three in the morning; the farm labourer was ready for his breakfast at eight o'clock, having already been at work since daybreak, and other people looked for some refreshment at the same hour.[5] In the mid-seventeenth century, Oliver Cromwell and his wife had a light broth for breakfast, as well as marrow pudding (sausages made with bone marrow and almonds).[6] Sir Kenelm Digby informs us that Queen Henrietta Maria also had a light broth in the morning, and he recommended as 'a wholesome course of diet' broth, or a cream of oatmeal or barley (a strained form of milk porridge) with two new-laid eggs for breakfast, adding with enthusiasm: 'Two poched eggs with a few fine dry-fryed Collops of pure Bacon, are not bad for breakfast, or to begin a meal.'[7]

By the eighteenth century, breakfast was established as a meal in well-to-do society. Lady Grisell Baillie directed that her daughter in 1705 breakfast at nine in the morning; dinner was between midday and two o'clock and supper came before her bedtime at nine o'clock.[8] At the end of the century, in 1786, another girl, Lord Sheffield's daughter, had breakfast at ten, dinner at four and supper as late as ten o'clock at night.[9]

The later dinner hour encouraged the development of breakfast as a meal, and it is especially noted in the context of the country house party. François de la Rochefoucauld, staying in England in 1784, commented that breakfast took place at nine o'clock, with tea and bread and butter, while in rich houses there was coffee and chocolate as well. The whole meal was comfortable and informal, and you could behave as if you were by yourself, in contrast to the formal evening dinner.[10]

Breakfast in the early years of the nineteenth century can be discerned in the novels of Jane Austen – several of her houses had breakfast rooms which provided a quiet place of refuge at other times of the day; and Northanger Abbey boasted a set of Staffordshire breakfast china. The greatest indication of what might have been consumed in such rooms is given in *Mansfield Park* (1814, Chapter 11) where we are told that William Price ate pork chops and mustard in contrast to Mr Crawford's boiled eggs, before they set off on a journey.

Anne Cobbett, in *The English Housekeeper*, which went through several editions in the first half of the nineteenth century, advised punctual and fixed hours for meals, especially breakfast, as the day's work commenced from that point; she also noted that late dinners had done away with hot suppers.[11] This might have been one reason for an interesting link between eighteenth-century suppers and the later nineteenth-century breakfast: one 'Bill of fare for Suppers' in 1759, given in Anne Battam's *Lady's Assistant*, includes cold meat, eggs and bacon, boiled and poached eggs, steaks, chops, potatoes and fish;[12] and Charlotte Mason in her *Lady's Assistant* of 1775 suggested family suppers including poached eggs on toast, sausages, cold meat and fried fish.[13] If hot suppers were being displaced by later dinners, it is not surprising to find these items being carried over to the next morning's breakfast which had come to replace the early dinner. The way was open for the development of the Victorian breakfast.

VICTORIAN WRITERS AND BREAKFAST FARE

By the beginning of Victoria's reign we already have evidence for most of the traditional ingredients: eggs, roasted, poached, or boiled; bacon; sausages; porridge, or cream of oatmeal; fish; pork chops; cold meats; bread and butter. Ale, beer and wine were giving way to tea, coffee and chocolate. The Victorians expanded the choice as through the developments of the Industrial Revolution they grew more prosperous, with affluence linked to the better transport of goods and ingredients.

Queen Victoria reigned from 1837 to 1901, but the flowering of the Victorian breakfast can best be seen in the period from about 1860 to the beginning of the First World War. It was of course a meal best enjoyed in the company of the well-to-do and the inhabitants of the country house, where affluence was linked to the leisure to enjoy the meal, but some note will be taken here of breakfasts in poorer households.

The first edition of Mrs Beeton's *Book of Household Management* in 1861 devotes only three paragraphs to 'the comfortable meal called breakfast', but these do summarize the range of the meal by this time. Cold meat, ham and tongue, collared and potted meats or fish, cold game or poultry, and veal-and-ham or game pies could be placed on the sideboard. Suggestions for hot dishes are broiled fish, mutton chops and rumpsteaks, kidneys, sausages, bacon, ham, poached and boiled eggs, omelettes, muffins, toast, butter and marmalade. Further information can be found in individual recipes, and the instructions on how 'To boil eggs for Breakfast' are accompanied by a picture of an egg-stand for the breakfast table.[14] Subsequent editions of *Household Management* trace the establishment of breakfast. Samuel Beeton's 1869 edition, after his wife's death in 1865, 'infused some new and modern information which seven years ago, did not exist',[15] and alterations and additions continued in subsequent editions by another publisher. By the 1880 edition, 'still further improvements' included new coloured illustrations and engravings, and in the appendix a new section, 'From Breakfast till Suppertime', included 'The Breakfast-table' and 'Little Breakfasts for the Family'.[16] The 1888 edition reflected the advances and new methods in cookery, and added to the original recipes, including some for vegetarians. New illustrations and coloured plates were introduced, and there was an expanded section on 'Breakfasts, Luncheons, Dinners, Teas and Suppers'. Chapter LX provides 'General Observations on Breakfast', with 'Menus for Wedding, Guest and Family Breakfasts'.[17]

Meanwhile, other books had been published devoted to breakfasts alone. *The Breakfast Book* of 1865 indicates the wide range of fare permitted. The first chapter gives 'the principal viands which are more or less in daily request for our ordinary breakfasts'; these include brawn, cold boiled beef, game, or poultry, ham, pickled pork and tongue; curries and devilled bones; bacon; eggs, including omelettes and fried eggs; eggs and bacon, and fried potatoes and bacon; beefsteaks, mutton chops — which, with the exception of sheep's kidneys, are 'the most generally consumed for breakfast' — pork chops and veal cutlets; fish, including bloaters and anchovies; and pies; accessories include marmalade, preserved fruit, or honey. Other chapters deal with made dishes such as croquettes, ham toast, hashed game and rissoles; sauces; savoury pies; savoury puddings, sausages, galantines and meat in jelly; and collared and potted meat. Fish, earlier described as 'an important adjunct to the breakfast table', has a chapter to itself, with another on fish pies and patties. Some fare was looked down on, however: 'Black puddings are not bad in their way, but they are not among the things we would make to set before our friends.'[18]

Another book dealing with the subject is *Breakfasts, Luncheons, and Ball Suppers* by Major L. . ., which appeared in 1887. He too had decided views on what was suitable:

The Author has always heard that the late Sir Tatton Sykes frequently breakfasted on 'apple tart', washed down by 'home-brewed ale'. *Chacun à son goût.* He doubts very much if it was frequently, if there is any truth in the legend at all; and although he feels the greatest respect for the memory of this most worthy and excellent of baronets, he has not put such a Bill of Fare amongst his menus. Any one caring to try such a breakfast must cater for himself.[19]

TYPES OF BREAKFAST

Breakfasts could be served in several degrees of formality and size. *The Breakfast Book* gives four types:

7

The family breakfast: hors d'oeuvres, or by-dishes, hot or cold, were served without sauce.

Déjeuner à la fourchette: the items were introduced in courses, similar to dinner.

Cold collation: 'almost all *recherché* things are proper for them, provided they are prepared for the purpose, so as to produce an ornamental effect.'

The ambigu: 'is an entertainment of a very heterogenous character, having resemblance to a dinner, only that everything is placed upon the table at once; and *relevés*, soup, vegetables, and hot *entremets*, are held to be ineligible. Our every-day breakfasts are in a small way served *en ambigu*, inasmuch as broiled fish, cold pasties, devilled bones, boiled eggs, cold ham, etc., all appear together.'[20]

Major L. . . divided his consideration of the meal into three chapters:

1. Breakfasts for Large Parties
2. Breakfasts for Ladies and Men of Sedentary Habits and Pursuits
3. Breakfasts for Sportsmen and those of active habits

The country-house breakfast should contain a variety of items to suit all the tastes of the guests, and he suggested:

fish, poultry or game, if in season; sausages, and one meat of some sort, such as mutton cutlets, or fillets of beef; omelets, and eggs served in various ways; bread of both kinds, white and brown, and fancy bread of as many kinds as can be conveniently served; two or three kinds of jam, orange marmalade, and fruits when in season; and on the side-table, cold meats, such as ham, tongue, cold game, or game pie, galantines, and in winter a round of spiced beef.[21]

Sportsmen and those with perfect health can manage to eat what they like and need no direction, but ladies, and men of sedentary habits, should take more care:

Ladies as a rule are much wiser, much more abstemious, and capable of practising much more self-denial in the feeding business than the male sex . . . they rarely, too, eat meat for breakfast . . . men who take no exercise, or who are over fifty years of age, should, if they wish to preserve their health . . . never eat meat more than once a day. . . . All meat will therefore be excluded from the Bills of Fare.[22]

His definition of meat is however limited, for the suggested fare, of three dishes with bread, buns, jam, etc., includes: ham omelette, poached eggs and ham, sausages, broiled chicken, sauté of kidney, roast lark, broiled ducklings and devilled turkey; and cold ham, tongue, poultry, game pies, galantines, brawn and game are on the side-table.[23]

THE GOOD BREAKFAST

Mrs Beeton in 1861 and *The Breakfast Book* in 1865 set a standard that was not always adhered to by the Victorians, for later writers were continually having to encourage them to choose more than bacon and eggs. Perhaps the 1880 edition of Mrs Beeton is not the best place to look for advice, although the new appendix had a chapter on 'The Breakfast Table', for it suggests only 'Breakfast dishes are usually cold joints, hot nick-nacks, and potted meats. Australian meats are also admissible, turned out of their tins, garnished and served cold.' 'Little Breakfasts for the Family' consists of menus for economical breakfasts, using leftovers from the day before rehashed in sauce or gravy, and occasionally adding eggs, fish, or bacon. To serve eggs and bacon every day could become too expensive for some households.[24]

Major L. . . had decided standards, although he too warned against extremes:

He thinks the reader will agree with him that as a rule, in England, breakfast is not sufficiently considered; that a good breakfast is the exception and not the rule, and that one sees either an *embarras de richesses* in the shape of pounds of mutton chops, beefsteaks, kidneys, and the ever-lasting (although excellent, if the eggs are fresh and the bacon good) eggs and bacon; or, on the other hand, barely sufficient of the over-night's repast, hashed or bedevilled, to satisfy half the party.[25]

He introduced a division into the study of the *British* breakfast:

He cannot understand why England should be so behindhand in the requirements necessary to the comfort of this meal. In Scotland it is quite a different thing; good breakfasts are the rule, not the exception. Only travel to Scotland, and arrive at Perth Station; in the refreshment room you see it at once: excellent fish, excellent meats, excellent jams, and bread and rolls of all sorts; and so it is in nearly all houses and in many hotels.[26]

It may be that writers needed to denigrate the English meal in order to encourage people to buy their books to remedy the situation. The 1888 edition of Mrs Beeton's *Book of Household Management* in the new chapter on breakfasts, seems to be doing the same thing:

Some one has said that English people do not know how to appreciate this meal, and there are certainly many who aver that they either do not care for it or cannot eat it, but we venture to suggest that if the former were to contrive to have more variety in the dishes served with this meal, and the latter were to make quite sure that no late hours or gaiety made them disinclined for it, both might find better appetites.[27]

Yet again, people are exhorted to soar above the national standard of eggs and bacon, and the chapter goes on to suggest two menus, and explain how the breakfast table should be laid.

Certainly those Victorians who bought recipe books had no lack of suggestions, often relating to the time of year. *The Breakfast Book* gave bills of fare for breakfasts for either eight to ten people or ten to twelve people for each quarter of the year, as shown in the following 'Spring Quarter' example (*The Breakfast Book* (1865), p. 129):

11

Spring Quarter.

BREAKFAST FOR 10 OR 12 PERSONS.

———

Middle of the Table.

Ribs of Beef, rolled.

———

4 By-dishes, Cold.

Pickled Oysters. Shrimps.

Radishes.   Plovers' Eggs, *à la cocque.*

———

2 Dishes of Cold Meat

A piece of Salmon, *au bleu.*   A Bayonne Ham, glazed.

———

4 By-dishes, Hot.

Russian Caviare, tossed.   Croquettes of Fish.
Sheep's Kidneys, grilled.   Small patties of Chicken.

———

4 Entrées.

Mayonnaise of Turbot.   Blanquette of Lamb.
Raised Pie of Pigeons.   Fillets of Mackerel, broiled.

———

Accessories as usual.

Henry Southgate, providing his account of *Things a Lady Would Like to Know*, said good tea, coffee or cocoa, bread and butter, and milk and cream were essential to all his suggested menus, one for each month of the year; 'September' and 'October' are shown in the example below (Henry Southgate, *Things a Lady Would Like to Know* (1881), p. 426):

SEPTEMBER

Broiled Haddock – Potted Ham – Sheeps' Tongues – Pig's Cheek – Cold Roast Fowl – Ham – Cold Grouse – Rolled Tongue – Cold Partridges – Scalloped Cod – Kippered Salmon.

OCTOBER

Giblet Pie – Cold Soles – Hot Sausages and Toast – Pigeon Pie – Bloaters and Boiled Eggs – Savoury Omelet – Potted Shrimps – Fried Whitings – Partridge Pie – Pheasant Pie – Kippered Salmon.

Major L. . . in 1887 gave four suggestions of 'Breakfasts for Large Parties' for each month of the year, indicating in later chapters how these could be amended for other types. He also added that tea, coffee and cocoa, brown and white bread, hot rolls, toast, muffins, fancy bread and buns, jam and fruit were part of each bill of fare. Here is 'April' (Major L. . ., *Breakfasts, Luncheons, and Ball Suppers* (1887), p. 7):

APRIL

Coquilles of Salmon.
Devilled Sausages.
Stewed Kidneys.

Mutton Cutlets.
Bouchées of Eggs aux Truffes.

————

Sole à la Colbert.
Kidney Omelet.
Dry Curry of Mutton.
Broiled Ham.
Eggs.

————

Broiled Whiting.
Dry Curry of Salmon.
Devilled Chicken.
Mutton Cutlets.
Poached Eggs.

————

Twice Laid of Cod.
Omelet aux Fines Herbes.
Sauté of Kidneys.
Beefsteak, Potato Ball.
Eggs.

————

COLD MEATS ON SIDE-TABLE.
Ham. Tongue. Galantine of Guinea Fowl in Aspic.
Boned Turkey. Silver Side of Beef.

Encouragement towards variety continued. M.L.
Allen produced *Breakfast Dishes for Every Morning of
Three Months* in 1884, and the twenty-fourth edition
came out in 1915. She was trying to avoid the

monotony of boiled eggs, bacon, dried fish, or sausages.[28] The following are two examples for March (M.L. Allen, *Breakfast Dishes for Every Morning of Three Months* (1884; 14th edn 1892), pp. 18–19):

MARCH 11TH, SUNDAY
Fried skate and shrimp sauce.
Curried pigs' feet.
Breakfast cakes.
Potted anchovy.
Devilled hot meat.
Hot buttered toast.
Jam.

MARCH 14TH, WEDNESDAY
Hard-boiled eggs, white sauce, and parsley.
Tomatoes baked.
Ham toast.
Periwinkle patties.
Scones.
Honey.

In 1894 Colonel A. Kenney Herbert, another military man whose service in India is reflected in his recipes, added another *Fifty Breakfasts* to the choice available. His menus were for families of six, and each included fish, meat and eggs, along with bread; many dishes were *réchauffé*, which meant that they could be prepared the previous evening. Here are four examples (A. Kenney Herbert, *Fifty Breakfasts* (1894; 4th impression 1904), pp. 13, 34, 47 and 98):

MENU II.
Fresh herrings au gratin.
Hashed mutton with fried bacon.
Omelette with herbs.
Scones.

MENU IX.
Fish Pudding.
Cold meat cutlets, with grilled bacon.
Eggs with anchovies.
Wholemeal cakes.

MENU XIV.

ABSTINENCE

Khitchri (Indian).
Macaroni à la Livornaise.
Eggs in white sauce.
Sally Lunns.

MENU XXXV.
Haddock in a mould.
Chicken cutlets, Indian way.
Eggs on the dish with bacon.
Crumb-muffins.

It can be seen that suggestions for a Victorian breakfast range from the modest to the opulent. The cookery books show that ideally the choice could have been far larger than the staple fare of bacon, sausages and eggs. The constant encouragement offered by writers from Mrs Beeton to Kenney Herbert and beyond may in fact have been necessary; the variety displayed in their books is delightful to contemplate, but may rarely have been a reality on the Victorian breakfast table.

The actual diet of a range of families at the end of Queen Victoria's reign was recorded from the notes they kept for a survey, published by B. Seebohm Rowntree in *Poverty: A Study of Town Life.* He divided his subjects into three classes: those with weekly earnings under 26 shillings; those with earnings over 26 shillings; and the servant-keeping class. Under these headings menus of all meals eaten were listed for the period of a week. A labourer, his wife and five children aged 2 to 11, with a weekly wage of 17s 6d, had the following breakfasts during the week ending 12 January 1900:

Friday	–	Bacon, bread, butter, coffee and cocoa
Saturday	–	Bacon, bread, coffee
Sunday	–	Bacon, bread, coffee, cocoa
Monday	–	Bacon, bread, dripping, coffee, cocoa
Tuesday	–	Bacon, bread, dripping, coffee, cocoa
Wednesday	–	Bacon, bread, coffee, cocoa
Thursday	–	Bacon, bread, dripping, coffee, cocoa[29]

On the Friday and Tuesday, the bacon provided the only meat of the day and Sunday gave the family its most elaborate dinner, of beef, potatoes and rice pudding. Another labourer with 25 shillings weekly and three children aged between 2½ and 8 had meat for dinner, tea, or supper on all days in the week ending 22 February 1901, which may have been the reason the family had bacon for breakfast only on Friday, Saturday and Sunday, making do with bread and butter or toast and dripping on the other days.[30]

In Class 2, a railway employee earning 44 shillings

a week, with two children aged 10 and 12, and a lodger, had the following breakfasts in the week ending 28 June 1901:

Friday   – Bacon, eggs, bread, cake, cocoa, tea
Saturday   – Bacon, eggs, bread, butter, cocoa, tea
Sunday   – Sausage, bread, butter, tea
Monday   – Bacon, eggs, bread, butter, tea
Tuesday   – Bacon, bread, butter, cake, tea
Wednesday   – Bacon, bread, butter, cake, tea
Thursday   – Ham, eggs, bread, butter, cake, tea[31]

This household regularly enjoyed a full cooked dinner, tea with some cheese, fish, or eggs, and a supper.

One of the servant-keeping families, of five adults and two children, showed its social standing by organizing its meals as breakfast, lunch, tea and dinner; apart from the regular bread, marmalade, hot milk and tea, the family had either bacon, eggs, or fish for their breakfast.[32] A final family in this third class, of six adults, had breakfast, dinner, tea and supper; their breakfasts during the week ending 4 March 1901 consisted of:

Friday   – Porridge, fried bacon, toast, bread,
              butter, marmalade, coffee
Saturday   – Porridge, fried bacon, toast, bread,
              butter, marmalade, coffee
Sunday   – Cold ham, toast, bread, butter,
              marmalade, coffee
Monday   – Porridge, cold ham, pork pie, toast,
              bread, butter, marmalade, coffee
Tuesday   – Porridge, fried bacon, potted beef,
              bread, toast, marmalade, tea

Wednesday   –   Porridge, fried bacon, eggs, toast,
                bread, marmalade, coffee
Thursday   –   Porridge, fried bacon, bread, toast,
                butter, marmalade, coffee[33]

Breakfasts actually eaten in the world outside cookery books remained faithful to the basics of bacon and eggs despite decades of advice from the cookery writers; even the better-off showed little variety.

Going to the top of the social scale, it is possible to see what the royal family ate through the revelations of one of their chefs, Gabriel Tschumi. He had come as a youth from Switzerland to work in the kitchens at Windsor Castle, and his first experience of a British breakfast was a surprise to him after his continental upbringing. At 7.00 a.m. he found the kitchen busy, with cooks roasting chops, cutlets, steaks, bloaters, sausages, chickens and woodcock, and preparing bacon rashers and egg dishes.[34] Of course, as throughout history, the royal kitchens were providing for a large household. Queen Victoria did not necessarily share in the full range, and Tschumi reported:

> Towards the end of her life she was not a large eater. Rumour had it that her breakfast was usually a boiled egg, served in magnificent style. According to the upper servants, she used a gold egg-cup and a gold spoon, and two of her Indian servants, in their showy scarlet and gold uniforms, stood behind her chair in case she wanted anything.[35]

The rest of her family would have eggs, bacon, fish, cutlets, chops or steak, roast chicken or other fowl, and the servants could have a similar number of courses.

Some of them often pocketed two or three hard-boiled eggs to help them through to the next meal.

THE APPEARANCE OF THINGS

The magnificence of Queen Victoria's egg-cup was reflected in the advice given to her subjects on the presentation of the breakfast table and items of food. *The Breakfast Book* pointed out that even the *recherché* dishes could produce an ornamental effect, that raised pies 'should invariably be served upon a damask napkin folded under them in the dish',[36] and fried fish 'should always be served upon a white napkin folded at the bottom of the dish and garnished with either sliced lemon or crisp parsley'.[37] One of the *Things a Lady Would Like to Know*, according to Henry Southgate, was that there should be a fair damask cloth on the breakfast table.[38] Mrs Beeton's original advice, in the 1861 edition of *The Book of Household Management*, was to have a vase of freshly gathered flowers on the table in summer, and a nicely arranged dish of fruit, with strawberries when in season, grapes or currants.[39] By the 1880 edition, it was also suggested that 'it is a graceful offering to your guests to lay beside, or in, their plates a tiny bouquet of sweetly smelling, if simple, flowers', and the simplicity extended to the china:

Let the breakfast set be neat and tasteful; there is nothing handsomer, nor better looking, nor neater, than the plain gold-edged white service our grandmothers liked to see. Gay breakfast services, that is to say, brilliant, gaudy sets, are entirely out of place.[40]

It is obvious that at this time tastes were changing, and in the 1888 edition, in the chapter on breakfasts, it was agreed that the china should be neat and tasteful, but the rest of the paragraph was dropped; hardly surprising, when an accompanying colour plate shows a selection of decidedly gaudy breakfast and tea china.[41]

WHAT TO DRINK

Ale at breakfast, recorded at the medieval and Tudor courts, may sound amusing now, but the alternative would have been wine or distilled water, for water on its own had to be used with care, depending on its source. It was the Victorians who provided piped clean water to every home, an essential undertaking in the age of industrial pollution and rapidly expanding cities. By the end of the nineteenth century, Major L. . . could chide Sir Tatton Sykes for enjoying his traditional home-brewed ale, and recommend instead tea, coffee, or cocoa. Each of these drinks merits study in its own right; their introduction into England marks the expansion of foreign trade that led to the formation of the British Empire, which in turn influenced the development of the British breakfast by introducing new foodstuffs, as well as creating greater affluence. A brief look at tea will provide an illustration.[42] Originally obtained from China and shipped to England, it was an expensive item and a curiosity in the seventeenth century when Pepys recorded his first taste,[43] being offered for between 16 shillings and 50 shillings a pound. This high cost led to some unscrupulous persons offering adulterated tea for sale, despite various Acts of Parliament during the eighteenth century forbidding such practices. G.G. Sigmond, Professor of Materia Medica to the Royal Medico-Botanical Society, in his treatise on *Tea: Its Effects, Medicinal and Moral*, described some prosecutions made by the Board of Excise in 1828, when evidence was produced of the adulteration of tea with the leaves of the white and black thorn trees, ash, sloe and elder. The resulting publicity caused respectable tea merchants, led by Mr Richard Twining, to emphasize the purity of their products and to press for the prosecution of those carrying out such fraud. Reference was also made to tea adulterated with deadly nightshade, ivy leaves, potato leaves, sage, or wheat husks, while verdigris and copperas were both employed to dye these spurious leaves.[44] It was obviously necessary to be able to recognize adulterated products, and Henry Southgate, before he gave directions for making tea, described how to distinguish genuine tea from sloe leaves: this was done by infusing the tea, making it possible to tell the narrower tea leaves from the rounded sloe leaves.[45]

Cheaper tea became available once the Assam tea fields were developed from a native plant found in that area, which fared better than the plants smuggled out of China. When Dr Sigmond wrote his treatise in 1839, this process was only just beginning; but he predicted that 'The tea of Assam may be obtained at a cheap rate, when once the establishments for its growth and preparation are placed upon a proper footing'.[46] The benefits of cheaper tea and its consequent availability to all classes of society took a little time to become established. Anne Cobbett advised in *The English Housekeeper* of 1851 that tea, like sugar and wine, should be kept locked up to remove temptation from the servants: 'Little pilferings at the tea-chest, perhaps, have been the beginning of that which has ended in depriving a poor girl of her character, and, consequently, of all chance of gaining her bread by honest means.'[47] By the end of the century this had changed, and Kenney Herbert, advocating tea with his *Fifty Breakfasts* in 1894, could afford to be generous in his instructions:

> The practice of doling out tea by carefully measured teaspoonfuls (handed down to us by our elderly maiden aunts) was perhaps necessary in the days when the only leaf in the market came from China and cost from four to five shillings a pound. The required strength was then obtained by the pernicious system of setting the tea 'to draw'. People now, however, have come to understand that to be wholesome tea must be produced by rapid infusion, not by a long process of steeping, and in order to get this at its best a good allowance of the leaf is necessary.[48]

CONCLUSION

The traditional items of the British Breakfast – bacon and eggs, sausages and fish – have been popular for several centuries. Porridge, the staple of the farm labourers and servants, remains associated with Scotland. Evidence for accompaniments, such as tomatoes and mushrooms, arrives with the Victorian recipe books, and certainly the bills of fare they suggest brought all the ingredients together and made breakfast a formal meal with its own etiquette. Several writers attempted to expand on the basic bacon and eggs, and encouraged more diverse items. Cooked meats included beefsteaks or mutton chops; rehashed meat, such as rissoles, and devilled bones were recommended, especially as they could be prepared in advance; fish was an important item; cold joints, galantines, potted meats and pies could adorn the sideboard. More exotic items include Bombay Duck, calf's head, cowheel, eel patties, pickled mussels, oysters and even reindeer's tongue. By the later nineteenth century, tinned meat was being used, although it still had to be nicely presented and garnished. Stewed apple or rhubarb and apricot or gooseberry fool are also to be found on menus, but these seem to be for children (although Sir Tatton Sykes's apple tart should not be forgotten). Up to twenty items were suggested for a country-house breakfast menu. The Victorian breakfast, in fact, was presented as a far more varied meal than the traditional concept of the British Breakfast, and writers such as Major L. . ., Colonel Kenney Herbert and their contemporaries are worthy of study. It is probable that many families, even those with the means to make a choice, continued to favour the basic items, and the recipe books are giving us a distorted picture of the actual practice, but the ideal is there.

The variety of fare continued through the Edwardian era, but the First World War marked the end of the true glory of the British Breakfast. Rationing was imposed even at Buckingham Palace, much to the disgust of the household servants; and after the war the earlier extravagance does not seem to have returned. Continental and American influences become apparent, with grapefruit, orange juice, cornflakes and muesli adding to and even ousting the traditional fare. But even though many people now eat only a continental-style breakfast – a roll and coffee – a 'real' breakfast is always enjoyed at weekends, or when on holiday.

The Great British Breakfast did not materialize overnight to greet the accession of Queen Victoria; but the Victorian achievement was to establish it as an acknowledged – and peculiarly British – meal.

APPENDIX TO CHAPTER ONE

RECIPES

A flavour of the Victorian breakfast – and of the cookery writers' style – can be glimpsed in the recipes for the basic items.

EGGS

To boil eggs for breakfast, salads, &c.

Eggs for boiling cannot be too fresh, or boiled too soon after they are laid; but rather a longer time should be allowed for boiling a new-laid egg than for one that is three or four days old. Have ready a saucepan of boiling water; put the eggs into it gently with a spoon, letting the spoon touch the bottom of the saucepan before it is withdrawn, that the egg may not fall, and consequently crack. For those who like eggs lightly boiled, 3 minutes will be found sufficient; 3¾ to 4 minutes will be ample time to set the white nicely; and, if liked hard, 6 to 7 minutes will not be found too long. Should the eggs be unusually large, as those of black Spanish fowls sometimes are, allow an extra ½ minute for them. Eggs for salads should be boiled from 10 minutes to ¼ hour, and should be placed in a basin of cold water for a few minutes; they should then be rolled on the table with the hand, and the shell will peel off easily.

Isabella Beeton, *The Book of Household Management* (1861), p. 824

To boil

Eggs to be good should not be more than two days old; after that they lose the creamy substance over the yolk which makes an egg so delicious. A new-laid egg takes a minute longer to boil than one which has been laid some days, and if you wish the white set it should be put in boiling water and allowed to boil four minutes and a half. If you prefer the white running all over your plate, and dropping all over your dress on the way to your mouth, let it boil three minutes and a half.

Major L. . . , *Breakfasts, Luncheons, and Ball Suppers* (1887), p. 72

Eggs to fry

Melt a piece of butter in a frying-pain, and slip the eggs in. – Or: lay some thin slices of bacon (not affected with rust), in a dish before the fire, to toast; break the eggs into tea-cups, and slip them gently into fresh boiling lard, in a frying-pan. When done, which will be in a little more than two minutes, lay each one (first trimming the white) on a slice of the bacon. Make a sauce of a little weak broth, cayenne, made mustard and vinegar.

Anne Cobbett, *The English Housekeeper* (c. 1840), p. 218

BACON

Frizzled bacon

Rashers, whether of bacon or ham, are quite an English institution; you will never even meet with the mention of them in Continental cookery-books. The meat should on no account be cut thick, and pains should be taken that it should be done to such a degree as to eat somewhat crisp, the fat being delicately browned. The most preferable way to dress it, is to toast it before the fire, either in a Dutch oven or in a bacon-toaster; but it is often broiled or tossed in a frying-pan.

The Breakfast Book (1865), pp. 11–12

SAUSAGES

Sausages

It is the usual practice to simply toss the sausages in lard or butter, for if broiled they are apt to become smoky before they are properly done. As they take some time to cook, first prick them with a needle to prevent the skins from breaking. Garnish with pickled red cabbage, or apples sliced and tossed till nicely browned. Observe that underdone sausages are execrable.

The Breakfast Book (1865), p. 19

PORRIDGE

Oatmeal porridge

This is a deservedly popular thing for breakfast. To prepare it, weigh a couple of ounces of oatmeal, put three-quarters of a pint of water in a saucepan, set it on the fire and bring it to the boil; cast into it a *pinch* (the eighth of an ounce) of salt, and then dredge in the oatmeal, stirring with a wooden spoon while the operation is being carried out. Simmer for forty minutes, by which time the oatmeal should have absorbed the water and be swollen and soft. It can now be served accompanied by a jug of hot milk, sugar or salt being added according to taste, the latter obviously for choice. Cream is, of course, a favourite adjunct with many, but does it not detract from the well-known wholesomeness of the porridge? I think so.

A. Kenney Herbert, *Fifty Breakfasts* (1894), pp. 150–1

FISH

Khitchri (Indian)

This dish, from which the so-called 'kedgeree' of English cookery books was doubtless taken, was originally a dish of rice cooked with butter and an Indian pea called *dál*, but now it may either be composed of cold cooked fresh fish, or of salt fish that has been soaked and either boiled or fried. Choose which you prefer – about one pound will be enough – and with a fork divide it into small pieces. Boil six ounces of rice. . . . These preparations can be made overnight. Boil three eggs hard, and with a fork crush them, whites and yolks together, to a coarse mince. Melt over a low fire three ounces of butter, and fry a very finely minced shallot therein till it is a yellow colour; now stir in the rice, using a wooden spoon, and the pieces of fish, season with pepper and salt and sufficient *turmeric* (about a teaspoonful) *to tint the rice a nice light yellow colour*; lastly, shake into the mixture the crushed hard-boiled eggs, and empty the whole into a very hot dish.

N.B. – Both onions and turmeric may be omitted, if it be desired, without prejudice to the mixture generally.

A. Kenney Herbert, *Fifty Breakfasts* (1894), pp. 47–8

ACCOMPANIMENTS

Mushrooms, broiled

Cut the stalks close to the heads of mushrooms well opened, take off the skin, put some small pieces of butter on each, sprinkle with pepper and salt, and arrange them in a baking tin, and cook in a Dutch oven before the fire; they should be cooked until soft, and put on buttered toast, and juice from them poured over them.

Major L. . ., *Breakfasts, Luncheons, and Ball Suppers* (1887), p. 131

Buttered eggs with tomatoes

Prepare the buttered eggs . . . and serve them hot from the stewpan upon a bed of tomatoes dressed as follows:–

Choose six moderately sized tomatoes; blanch them in scalding water for three minutes to facilitate the removal of the skin, which having been done, take a small stewpan, put half an ounce of butter into it with one finely sliced half-ounce shallot; fry till beginning to turn golden, then empty into the pan the whole of the tomatoes sliced thinly; stir round, and add a teaspoonful of coarsely ground black pepper (fresh from a table-mill for choice), a saltspoonful of powdered dry *basil*, and one of salt. Continue the stirring for ten minutes over a fairly brisk fire to prevent catching, and the tomatoes will be ready. A tablespoonful of white sauce, or the yolk of a raw egg, should be stirred in – off the fire – before final dishing up. It is quite unnecessary to pass this through the sieve. People fond of Continental cookery can direct that one clove of garlic be stewed with the tomatoes, uncut, to be picked out before serving.

A. Kenney Herbert, *Fifty Breakfasts* (1894), pp. 21–2

TWO

LUNCHEON, NUNCHEON AND RELATED MEALS

C. ANNE WILSON

Luncheon, also known as lunch, was already well established in the British Isles by the time Victoria became queen. But this form of refreshment was a relative newcomer as a named meal to fill the ever-widening gap between breakfast and dinner. Neither lunch nor luncheon appeared in books as definitions of this meal as part of the daily eating arrangements of the middle and upper classes before the beginning of the nineteenth century, though the words were no doubt in conversational use for a few years before they reached the printed page.

Dr William Kitchiner gave one of the early descriptions of luncheon and its role in the day's programme in his book *The Art of Invigorating and Prolonging Life*, the third edition of which was published in 1822. As might be expected from the title, he took a physician's view of the meal, advising a much lighter

repast than that put forward in cookery books a decade
or two later.

> The interval between Breakfast and Eleven o'clock
> is the best time for intellectual Business – then
> Exercise again till about Twelve, when probably the
> Appetite will be craving for a Luncheon which
> may consist of a bit of roasted Poultry, a basin of
> good Beef tea, or Eggs poached or boiled in the
> shell, Fish plainly dressed, or a Sandwich – stale
> bread – and half a pint of good Home-brewed
> Beer, or Toast and Water with about one-fourth or
> one-third part of its measure of Wine, of which
> Port is preferred.[1]

(Toast and water was made by pouring boiling water
over a slice of toasted bread, leaving it to infuse until
cool, then straining off the liquid. People argued
with passion as to whether the toast should be
pale brown or burned black;[2] but either way, this
drink would undoubtedly have been improved by an
addition of wine.) Dr Kitchiner continued: 'The solidity
of the Lunch should be proportionate to the time it is
intended to enable you to wait for your Dinner, and the
activity of the exercise you take in the meantime.' He
was writing for readers whose dinnertime had
advanced to 5.00 p.m.

But in the eighteenth and preceding centuries dinner
had been eaten at various earlier hours. This meant
that rather different forms of refreshment filled the gap
between breakfast and dinner, and between dinner and
supper. Such snack meals had their own names and
traditions. But they survived among some groups of
people to the very end of Queen Victoria's reign.

NUNCHEON AND BEVER

Among the interim snacks of medieval times 'nuncheon' is the one which sounds most likely to have been the forerunner of luncheon. In fact, the name was derived from two Anglo-Saxon words, *nōn* (pronounced like 'known') meaning noon or midday, and *shench* meaning drink. But this medieval predecessor of today's 'liquid lunch' was apparently always accompanied by bread, to judge from the fourteenth-century documents which provide our earliest evidence for it. Bread and ale were issued for the 'nonsenchis' of the sawyers working at King's Hall at Cambridge in 1342; and one loaf of bread plus one jug of ale each for 'nonshenches' to the workers at the convent at Abingdon in 1375.[3] The word 'nonshench' gradually turned into 'nuncheons', with a final 's' which did not drop out until the seventeenth century.

Nuncheons is recorded most often as a meal-break for manual workers. But we know that people of high social rank also expected light refreshment between main meals. All the upper servants in the great castles and houses of the aristocracy in late medieval times received daily liveries of ample quantities of wine and bread to take to their rooms, so that they could fortify themselves at any point during the day when they felt thirsty or hungry, and could also offer small-scale hospitality to visitors who paid them business or social calls. Middle- and lower-ranking servants were given liveries of ale and bread in smaller amounts, the quantities decreasing in proportion to their rank; but those who received the smallest rations were not expected to share them.

What name they gave to these informal little meals is

not clear, but it could well have been in the great houses that the word 'bever' was first used. Bever (pronounced 'beaver' and not as in the first two syllables of our word 'beverage') developed from the Old French *beivre*, which came in turn from Latin *bibēre*, meaning 'to drink'; and since Anglo-Norman French had lingered on in the names of the cooked dishes consumed on feastdays in great houses, and since the names of contemporary wines were nearly all of French origin, it would not be surprising if a French-derived term were used to describe a light refreshment in which the liquid element played an important part.

By 1500 bever was being used more generally to mean much the same as nuncheons. The noontime drink must originally have followed a dinner taken around ten o'clock in the morning or even earlier. As the hour for dinner grew later, the timing of nuncheons also had to change, and the records show that it moved forward to become an afternoon refreshment. In the case of the records of 1529 for the borough of Stirling, the timing of the meal-breaks is spelled out very carefully: the working man is to have on 'ilk werk day ane half hour afor nine houris afore none [i.e. from 8.30 to 9.00 a.m.] to his disjone [i.e. breakfast], and ane ither half hour afor four houris eftyr noon [i.e. from 3.30 to 4.00 p.m.] to his nunchenkis'.[4] 'Disjone' means to 'de-fast' or 'end fast' or 'break fast'; it too passed from late Latin into medieval French, and was then borrowed by the Scots. But whereas in Britain we have kept our breakfast as the first meal of the day, in France it has moved forward to become the noonday meal, and the day there now begins with '*petit déjeuner*'.

It is interesting to see that the working people of

Stirling after their disjone ended at nine o'clock had to continue their labours for a further six and a half hours before they had their next mealbreak of nuncheons. We may deduce that their final meal, when work was over for the day, was supper; and that they did not eat dinner except on special occasions.

Both nuncheon and bever were still being consumed at the beginning of the nineteenth century, and indeed survived to the end of Queen Victoria's reign. But nuncheon gradually slipped out of general speech to become a dialect word in places as far apart as Whitby, on the east coast of Yorkshire, and Wiltshire. According to the *Wiltshire Glossary* of 1893, 'About Salisbury Nuncheon is between 10.00 and 10.30 a.m. and again at 4.00 p.m. and is a very small meal'.[5]

Bever had become the word used for the workmen's mid-morning or mid-afternoon refreshment over a wide area of south-east England, the Midlands and East Anglia. William Ellis reported in 1750 on the seed cake made to supply 'beaver victuals' to the harvest workers in Hertfordshire 'about four of the clock in the afternoon with some cheese, for the Harvest-men to eat this Cake dry with, or to dip it in Ale'.[6]

In the nineteenth century, the day's timetable for Hertfordshire labourers began with first breakfast before 6.00 a.m. followed by breakfast or 'eight o'clock' at 8.00 a.m. and bever at 10.00 or 11.00 a.m.,[7] thus breaking up the working day into much shorter stretches than the 6½-hour stint of the Stirling workers three centuries earlier. The bever also lingered on as a refreshment break in public schools such as Eton, Winchester and Charterhouse; and here, too, it could be either a mid-morning or a mid-afternoon break. The drink was always beer, accompanied by bread or bever-cake, a plain, solid yeasted cake with just a few currants. When the bever was abolished at Eton in 1890, its passing was noted in the *Saturday Review*, and was no doubt mourned by many Old Etonians.[8]

One reason why both nuncheon and bever finally died out could have been the increasing use of tea, and later coffee, as drinks between meals. They fulfilled a similar function, but they were 'new' drinks compared with the long-established nuncheon and bever of ale or beer. But the tea-break and coffee-break took a surprisingly long time to arrive, at least under those names: according to the *Oxford English Dictionary* they did not appear in print until the late 1940s. A rather interesting extension of the meaning of bever was recorded by Henry Mayhew in his book, *London Labour and the London Poor*, first published in 1851. Among Londoners, he said, '*all* beer, brandy, water or soup are "beware"'.[9] Again, there is no mention of tea, although the cheapest teas were by then widely consumed among London's working people.

LUNCHEON AND LUNCH

So much for the liquids. Now we come to the solid part. 'Luncheon' makes its first appearance on the English side of a French-English dictionary of 1580, where the French *lopin* is translated as 'a lumpe, a gobbet, a luncheon'. Fynes Moryson in his *Itinerary* of 1617 wrote of 'eating a great lumpe of bread and butter, with a luncheon of cheese.' Ralph Thoresby of Leeds, in a letter of 1703 to John Ray, referred to 'a huge lunchin of bread', again meaning a lump. In the meantime, soon after luncheon and apparently quite independently, 'lunch' had arrived. 'Lunch' is first recorded in a Spanish-English dictionary, where *lonja de tocino* is translated as 'a lunch of bacon'.[10] The usage of lunch to mean a slice continued to the end of the eighteenth century, and luncheon continued to mean gobbet for nearly as long.

But gobbets and slices of bread and cheese or bacon were in fact the materials for a light meal. In the 1650s one writer referred to 'noonings and intermealiary lunchings', and another to 'afternoon lunchins';[11] and they both seem to be using 'lunchings' to mean approximately the same as nuncheons.

Edward Ward published in the early 1700s a mock-heroic poem called *The Bloodless Battle* about the London trainbands, which included the following rather ambiguous couplet:

Then others more hungry, their stomachs to please
Sat down to their luncheons of household and cheese.

('Household' was the type of everyday bread eaten by servants and labourers.) But it turns out that this is not 'luncheon' in the later sense of the word. The men of the trainbands had set out carrying not only their equipment but also quantities of 'food to preserve 'em'; and had already been treated to a large dinner shortly after twelve o'clock by the Lord Mayor. The luncheons the men ate were gobbets of bread and cheese, for the poet continued: 'Each bit they swallow's as big as my Fist'.[12] It was still to be some time before luncheon, in our sense of the word, came to the fore.

Meanwhile something else was happening to affect the organization and naming of meals. Dinner in the seventeenth century took place about one o'clock. But during the eighteenth century it slipped forward to two, then from two to three, and eventually to four or five o'clock. It is true that the contemporary breakfast, at least for the comfortably off, was a leisurely meal taken at ten o'clock in the morning. But by ten o'clock most people had been up and about for a couple of hours, engaged in various activities; and their breakfast of light breads, buns and wigs (wedgecakes) accompanied by coffee or chocolate was not always enough to sustain them for several more hours.

From Nooning to Lunch

For the ladies, those hours were often spent in visiting friends (while the menfolk saw to the business of their estates or their professions); and at first a glass of madeira and a slice of madeira cake could be enough to fill the gap. But as time went on, and dinner moved further forward, something a little more substantial seemed to be called for; and the name given to this refreshment was 'nooning'. Like 'lunchings', the word 'nooning' was first recorded in the 1650s. It is clearly connected with noon, the time of day when it was taken, and it had to be introduced because the older midday nonshench had now become nuncheon, a mid-morning or mid-afternoon refreshment for workpeople, who breakfasted earlier and had a longer working day than their employers.

Nooning was a well-established repast by the beginning of the nineteenth century. Among the general advice in the introduction to Mrs Rundell's *A*

New System of Domestic Cookery, first published in 1806, is the following:

> When noonings or suppers are served (and in every house some preparation is necessary for accidental visitors), care should be taken to have such things in readiness as are proper for either.[13]

This statement was repeated through the many later editions of Mrs Rundell's book, and remained unchanged in the 1849 edition, suggesting that the term nooning was still meaningful in the mid-nineteenth century. The words 'such things . . . as are proper for either' may be taken to indicate that the same type of food was served on either occasion. We know that suppers were smaller and more informal than dinners, and comprised such foods as cold meat, tongue, ham, potted meat or fish, pies and tarts, often laid out so that guests could help themselves, buffet-style, with perhaps a single hot dish. So Mrs Rundell's noonings were certainly much more substantial than a mere slice of bread or cake to accompany a drink.

The nooning also had to be available in adequate quantities to accommodate the unexpected guest or guests, because it was consumed at a point within the usual visiting hours during which ladies, sometimes accompanied by one or two other members of their families, called at the houses of their friends. Visiting hours from the later eighteenth century onwards had been from 11.00 a.m. to 3.00 p.m. or even 4.00 p.m. as the time for dinner moved forward.

Jane Austen's name for the midday repast was 'noonshine', mentioned twice in letters she wrote during 1808;[14] and here she seems to have combined the idea of 'nooning' with the old word 'nuncheon'. Possibly it was just a family usage, or a word in very limited circulation. But she and other people writing at this period were already beginning to use another term for a light meal taken between breakfast and dinner, and this was 'luncheon'. From the way it makes its first appearances in early nineteenth-century novels, it seems possible that the earlier concept of lunch or luncheon as a wedge of solid food of the bread and cheese variety, taken along by the eater to supply a light meal at an appropriate time, had been extended to cover food which people carried with them when they went to an inn. It was quite common for people to do this, and to eat their own provisions at the inn, having purchased the accompanying drink from the landlord.

In Jane Austen's *Pride and Prejudice*, published in 1813, Lydia and Kitty Bennett, waiting to meet their two elder sisters at the coaching inn, buy and bring in salad and cucumber which they prepare themselves, and add 'such cold meat as an inn larder usually affords', so as to make what Lydia later describes as 'the nicest cold luncheon in the world' to welcome the travellers.[15] Maria Edgeworth, in *The Absentee* of 1812, wrote about London maidservants visiting Ireland with their employers who take a picnic lunch with them to eat at the inn when they go off on their own on an excursion to a nearby village.[16]

Very soon, however, both 'lunch' and 'luncheon' became the names for a domestic meal, and although unexpected callers might join the family, it was also a meal for which definite invitations were issued. Both forms of its name, 'lunch' and 'luncheon', were used, more or less interchangeably, though there was a brief early period when 'lunch' became the fashionable version, and the committee of Almack's Club in 1829 decided that 'luncheon is avoided as unsuitable to the polished society there exhibited'[17] – exactly the reverse of the 'U' or upper-class society whose linguistic secrets Nancy Mitford revealed in the 1950s (when 'lunch' was non-U, and 'luncheon' was U).

Its timing was less elastic than that of dinner, and people usually began the meal at some point between 12.30 and 2.00 p.m. The authors of *The Complete Servant*, published in 1825, explain: 'About one o'clock the family generally take their lunch, and the servants their dinner.'[18] A third meal often had to be produced at that hour for the children, so the first duties of the kitchen maid or undercook after breakfast were concerned with 'preparing for the servants' dinner, the dinner in the nursery or elsewhere and the lunch in the parlour'. Furthermore, 'At lunch time, the cloth being laid by the under-butler or footman, it is the duty of the butler to carry the tray, or arrange the table, and when there is company, he waits in the room assisted by the other servants.' He also had to fetch wine or ale, as required.[19]

Thomas Webster's *Encyclopaedia of Domestic Economy* of 1844 assigns the luncheon duties to the 'sole footman', in those establishments boasting no more than one: 'The parlour luncheon being generally called for about one o'clock, he will usually be at liberty to get his tray ready; when carried into the parlour and properly arranged, he will usually be at liberty to get his own dinner which is generally at this time of day.'[20] Lunch or luncheon remained throughout the nineteenth century and beyond a meal for the comfortably-off classes. Webster's *Encyclopaedia* makes it plain that the one-servant family ate dinner as their midday meal, prepared, cooked and also served, after a change of apron, by the 'servant of all work', who herself dined afterwards 'on the remains of the dinner'.[21] And for members of the working population in general who ate a midday main meal, that meal was invariably dinner.

In the development of luncheon as a recognized middle-day meal there was topographical variation (it was adopted more readily in southern England than in regions further north); there was sexual differentiation (it was more popular with women than with men); and there was also something of a generation gap. The latter can be traced in Mrs Gaskell's novel, *North and South*, published in 1855.

The story begins when the Hale family are still living in a country rectory in the south of England. There Mrs Hale, flustered by the arrival of an unexpected guest, exclaims, 'It is most unfortunate. We were dining early today and having nothing but cold meat, in order that the servants may get on with their ironing.' Her daughter Margaret (who, significantly, has previously lived for some time at the more sophisticated London home of a cousin) consoles her with the reply, 'Papa likes Mr Lennox. . . . And never mind the dinner, dear mama. Cold meat will do capitally for a lunch, which is the light in which Mr Lennox will most likely look upon a two o'clock dinner.'[22]

When we examine more closely what is said about the luncheon-eating classes of the mid-nineteenth century, we find that the impetus for developing and maintaining this meal came largely from the women. Anne Bowman emphasized this in *The New Cookery Book* of 1867 where she wrote:

Luncheons, which are in fact the substantial meal for those who dine at a very late hour, may include cold meats of all kinds, game, fowls, ham, brawn, pâtés, broiled or hashed meats, soup, cutlets, mashed potatoes and even a pudding, with ale, porter or wine on the table. The lady of the house frequently makes her real dinner at luncheon.[23]

The same point was developed by Major L. . . in the 1880s in his book *Breakfasts, Luncheons, and Ball Suppers*. Under the heading 'Ordinary House Luncheons' he began: 'How to commence this chapter the Author hardly knows, this being the ladies' meal. . . . Sorry will he be if his bills of fare are not to their taste. Breakfast not being their meal, and dinner in *many cases* only very slightly patronized, nature demands, if health is to be repaired, that one meal in the day should be a substantial one. Why they select the middle of the day for this repast' he could not imagine; he hoped that 'perhaps some fair but kindly critic may enlighten him'.

The reason why he has embarked on luncheons at all becomes clearer when he moves on to the special menus for hunting luncheons, race luncheons, travelling luncheons and shooting luncheons. Here he describes the specially constructed hunting luncheon-case, which is to have a division, one side for the pie (a moist meat pie containing plenty of jelly) or cold cutlets, the other for bread, cake, or plum pudding; and the rather similar travelling luncheon basket of his own design, complete with a section to hold two pint bottles, one for champagne or claret, the other for sherry or Salutaris water, plus four cups of transparent horn fitting into each other, and pepper, salt, mustard, knives, forks, two plates 'and a portable table is fastened outside'.[24]

Among the leisured classes, and especially at their country homes, the house luncheon was in fact enjoyed by both sexes. The menu book of Glamis Castle, home of the Earls of Strathmore, for summer 1866 shows that luncheon parties were held more frequently than dinner parties, and that people from neighbouring houses were invited together with all their own house guests, resulting on several occasions in luncheons for twenty-two people.[25]

It was the professional and business men who were unwilling to adopt the midday luncheon, seeing it as an unwelcome interruption to working hours that had previously stretched unbroken across the middle of the day. As the century progressed, breakfasts were taken earlier, and the five o'clock dinner moved forward to six o'clock or later. But men clung to their old habits. It is recorded that Macaulay yielded only in 1853 and because of failing health to what he described as 'the detested necessity of breaking up the labours of the day by luncheon'.[26]

In the early 1880s, business and professional men, who by then were breakfasting at eight or nine o'clock, still, according to the compilers of *Cassell's Domestic Dictionary*,

too often make the mistake of omitting this mid-day meal and content themselves from the time they leave home in the morning to the dinner hour in the evening with a biscuit or some equally insignificant portion of food.

Such behaviour, they warned, quickly leads to great disorders of the nervous and digestive systems, and 'the remedy for these will be found in the neglected luncheon'.[27]

The same *Domestic Dictionary* advises on etiquette:

Precedence is not observed at an ordinary luncheon, nor do the gentlemen conduct the ladies to the room where it is laid. The hostess leads the way and the guests follow. Ladies may retain their bonnets and outdoor attire when invited to remain for luncheon.

The guests helped each other to the food, 'although it is sometimes arranged that servants should hand the plates of the first course and then leave the room'.[28]

LUNCHEON FARE AND DINNER FARE

Typical food for the luncheon menu has already been described, and most cookery books offered rather similar suggestions. Mrs Beeton, for instance, wrote: 'the remains of cold joints, nicely garnished, a few sweets or a little hashed meat, poultry or game are usual articles placed on the table for luncheons, with bread and cheese, biscuits, butter, &c.'[29]

The role of hashed meat, which appears on nearly all lists of luncheon fare, had been made clear several years earlier by Alexis Soyer. The opening chapters of his book *The Modern Housewife* took the form of a series of letters from the experienced Mrs B to her young friend Mrs L. Mrs B observed that the cold meats offered at luncheon were the roast joints of the previous dinner or dinners. They were well trimmed, 'for you must be aware that after four or five have dined from a leg of mutton, its appearance becomes quite spoiled, and looks blackish when cold'; and they were garnished, 'with a pretty little paper frill upon the knuckle' in the case of mutton or pork. The trimmings of beef, pork, mutton and also the pickings from the carcasses of game birds or poultry eaten at the previous dinner were duly hashed and reheated in a tasty gravy sauce; and Mrs B commented, 'I always remark that they never partake of any cold meat while any of the hash remains.'[30] And indeed at Glamis Castle too, the leftovers, in the form of hashed hare, minced mutton and eggs, and so forth were reserved for the luncheon menus.[31]

Mrs B added a tart or pudding, made along with the ones for the midday nursery dinner, and she timed her luncheon to begin at half past twelve. She could then claim that 'luncheon . . . scarcely increases my expenditure', being 'generally made up of the remains of dinner; and the remains of luncheon will dine our three servants at half past one'. In the summer she 'introduced a few dishes of fruit, and less meat'.[32] Ten years later, Mrs Beeton likewise recommended dishes of fresh fruit for summer luncheons, or fruit compotes, tarts or puddings. Needless to say, she has a recipe for luncheon cake, too.[33]

Mrs Beeton recorded one response to the fragmentation of the meal at the end of the morning which now occurred in middle-class households. 'In families where there is a nursery', she wrote, 'the mistress of the house often partakes of the meal with the children, and makes it her luncheon.'[34] Alternatively, older children were sometimes allowed to share the adult luncheon downstairs, even when guests were present.

But a large part of the working population continued to eat dinner after the morning's work, and many, especially those whose labours were physically demanding, also ate lunch. For them 'lunch' was a newer term for the traditional nuncheon or bever. The solid part, the hunk or 'lunch' of bread or cheese, had finally given its name to the entire snack (and for working people lunch continued to have the role of a between-meal snack). Once this happened, their employers borrowed the word to denote their own gradually expanding meal which bridged their greater gap between breakfast and dinner.

'The English labourer has his "lunch" between breakfast and dinner and again between the latter meal and supper', according to a medical authority quoted in *Cassell's Dictionary of Cookery* in the 1880s.[35] Beer or cider with bread and cheese or pieces of fairly plain cake were the usual components.

Servants also had a mid-morning lunch, though in mid- or late afternoon the indoor servants, at least, partook of the 'servants' tea', with bread and cakes, and tea as the accompanying beverage. They were not encouraged to linger over their lunch. Katharine Mellish wrote, at the very end of the Victorian era:

It is usual for servants to have lunch, either bread and cheese or a piece of cake, about eleven o'clock; but they should not be allowed to sit down to it, as the morning hours are too precious. The cook should see that this meal is expeditiously despatched. Beer (if allowed at all) should not be taken at this lunch-time.[36]

All through the twentieth century lunch has strengthened its hold as the meal for the middle of the day (luncheon is now reserved for the most formal occasions), extending to an ever-widening range of social groups. But it is not yet accepted universally. Many older people still eat their main meal of the day at that time, and still call it 'dinner', thus following a tradition that goes back through the Victorian era to the centuries before the Industrial Revolution.

THREE

PROLIFERATING PUBLICATIONS: THE PROGRESS OF VICTORIAN COOKERY LITERATURE

LYNETTE HUNTER

The primary question I want to address is a simple one. Why is there such a proliferation from the 1860s to the end of the century and beyond, of small books specifically on individual meals? Studying these and other related food and household books in the nineteenth century leads to the suggestion that the proliferation was made possible by printing technology and new systems of distribution, and that it mediated a radical change in the lives of middle-class women by which meals became the focus for a series of social gestures needed to alleviate the isolation of the private family.

Early nineteenth-century books related to food and cookery are most often single-authored comprehensive guides to household management, or edited selections from magazines or other works.[1] Because of the expense of these books which retailed for 10s 0d to £1 or more,[2] it is likely that they were aimed at the substantial middle-class housewife. The household guides are frequently addressed to the lady of the house whose main work revolved around the preserving, distributing and cooking of foodstuffs, whether she was in an urban or rural setting. In contrast to these books, many of which were written by women such as Maria Rundell, Mrs Dalgairns, or Eliza Acton, the edited selections were normally put together by men; for example, William Pybus's *A Manual of Useful Knowledge* (1810), J. Stewart's *The Young Woman's Companion* (1814), the anonymous *The New Female Instructor* (1820?), James Jennings's *The Family Encyclopedia* (1821), or Watkin Poole's *The Female's Best Friend* (1826). These selections seem to be more concerned with providing an educational base for the middle-class woman, and often include sections on 'conversation', on 'geography', on 'arithmetic', as well as on general household management, food and cookery.

However, if we jump fifty years, while there are still large compendious guides published by newspapers and magazines, such as *Cassell's Household Guide* (in editions from 1869 to 1912) or *'The Queen's' Cookery Books* (from 1896) by Mrs S. Beatty-Pownall, and by publishers, such as *Ward and Lock's Home Book* (1880) which was also issued under the title *Beeton's Household Treasury of Domestic Information*, or *Nelson's Home Comforts* (1882), the marked difference is in the dozens of single-authored food books directed towards specialized aspects of household management: courses, foodstuffs, dishes, technology, commercial products, and meals themselves. Mary Hooper's *Little Dinners* (1874) and Marian Harland's (Mrs Terhume's) *Breakfast, Luncheon and Tea* (1875) are among the early examples, shortly to be followed by books covering the use of baking powder or gelatine, cooking with gas or with pressure cookers, cooking with spices and unusual vegetables, and other books on meals, courses and dishes such as Isabella Thwaites's *Fish Cookery* (1883), Mary Allen's *Breakfast Dishes* (1884), Harriet Dwight's *Bread-making* (1884) and Rose Owen Cole's *Breakfast and Savoury Dishes* (1885). The list can be very full, but generally many writers such as Harriet de Salis, Charles Herman Senn, Arthur Kenney Herbert, Myrtle Reed (Olive Green), Mrs Alfred Praga, Dorothy Peel, Rose Brown and Mrs S. Beatty-Pownall, built careers around the publication of specialized books. Charles Senn alone produced more than thirty titles, often with ten editions of each, with probably at least 5,000 copies in each edition. A very conservative estimate of his output would be in the order of 1.5 million books; it is more likely to have been twice or three or more times this number.[3]

PUBLISHING BACKGROUND

So what happens in the central years 1840 to 1870? The large edited collections are the location for an important development in the history of book publication in Britain. While many of these books had been produced in the early decades of the century for a moneyed audience, a number of events occurred during the period 1840 to 1870 which meant that the potential audience for the material expanded enormously.[4] During the 1840s many of the political controls over printing presses were lifted,[5] and following the disintegration of the Chartist movement, taxes on newspapers, on advertisements, on paper, on rag supplies for paper, were successively lifted from 1852 to 1861. Robert Philp, a great Chartist publisher, is a clear example of a new kind of editor who made much of the situation. His periodical publications, *Home Companion*, *Family Tutor* and *Family Treasury*, contained the material that went into his best-selling *Enquire Within*[6] which ran to ninety-seven editions before the turn of the century, each edition being approximately 10,000 books. Philp not only exploited looser government controls and much cheaper untaxed production, but must also have made effective use of the sophisticated distribution system for newspapers established by the Chartists during the 1840s, which elaborated on the back of the railway system and the associated growth in bookstalls and bookshops that resulted.

One other important example of this development, which took it one stage further, is found in the work of Samuel Beeton. Beeton had started the *English Women's Domestic Magazine* in 1852, capitalizing in a manner similar to Philp on the changes in the printing and publishing world, and selling the magazine for only 2*d*.[7] But Beeton was particularly close to the new printing technology. His magazine for the middle-class and aspiring housewife, *The Queen*, coming out from the 1860s onwards, used the new techniques for graphic illustration and reproduction, and made much of the new rotary steam-press technology.[8] More interesting was Beeton's relationship with the publishers Ward, Lock & Tyler, later Ward, Lock & Company, centring around the publication and republication of Isabella

Beeton's *The Book of Household Management*. Initially brought out in monthly parts during 1858–60, *Household Management* probably achieved wide sales because it was therefore more affordable than Thomas Webster's *Encyclopaedia of Domestic Economy* (1844) from which the cookery at any rate was largely derived. In 1861, Beeton published the parts in one volume. However, subsequently, from about 1870, *Household Management* was not only republished and re-edited as a single volume but was split up and published in small parts, including *Beeton's Book of the Laundry*, *Beeton's Domestic Recipe Book*, *Beeton's Housekeeper's Guide*, etc. The success of these focused and often shorter books is coincident with the sudden proliferation of single-authored specialized books from the 1870s onwards.

Why did Beeton, with Ward, Lock & Tyler, choose to split up the larger collection? There are a number of issues which partially address the answer to this question. The growth in bookstalls and bookshops could mean that the casual purchaser was becoming more likely, but casual purchase means smaller and cheaper books: books that don't require a large and serious investment. However, in Britain there was no consistent production of paperback books, so small hardcover books in publishers' bindings emerged. At the same time, the magazine industry was expanding quickly and creating different attitudes in both writers and readers towards fashion and status.

Periodicals of all kinds, but especially those directed towards the middle-class woman, were driven by the commercial interests of advertisers. The goods on display were part of current marketing, often being sold as 'novelties'; the advertisers' main concern was that the magazine or periodical should create strategies for bringing the reader back to the next issue, the next novelty. And magazines responded with the interview with a famous person, with elaborate correspondence columns, with the regular serialized fiction, with dates of events and descriptions of society life: constructing ideas of desirable fashion and status to whet the appetite and sate the pleasure of their readers.[9]

Furthermore, to have retained the voluminous household book alone would have been impossible in face of the speed with which several aspects of life directly addressed by books on food and cookery, were changing. Where the technology of cookery had for most people remained largely the same for several hundred years, the second half of the nineteenth century saw the introduction of gas fires, gas refrigerators and cookers, electric cookers (in the last years) and associated devices; and where marketing, preservation and conservation had been central to the housewife's work for centuries, suddenly there were commercially bottled and canned foods,[10] and shops with unusual foreign foodstuffs, and pre-packaged foods. In order to address the different knowledge needed by this variety of change, printed material had to become more flexible: shorter and more specific books were essential.

There is also the direct involvement of the writer and reader in this complex and sophisticated set of social and commercial issues. Tied into these other developments and inextricably linked with changes in education that occurred during the 1840–70 period, culminating in the Education Acts of 1870 and 1876, was the increasing professionalization of authorship and the ever-expanding number of readers. Most printed household books had until the 1830s been directed towards the middle classes. But a literature of food and cookery did exist for popular dissemination, in pamphlets, circulated diaries, recipes in newspapers and the like. When in the 1850s sales broadened across all classes of earners/workers,[11] because books were cheaper and the standard of living was improving, a large audience that had been reading printed material was brought into the *book*-buying public. This readership was also more varied, and its needs asked for different kinds of book. At the same time, as writing became more respectable, and more pressure was put on effectively employing the Copyright Act, more people began to earn their living as writers. Often the work was divided between writing for the periodicals and writing single books; but whereas periodical writing was normally anonymous, the book was published conveying the name of the author. Many of the specialized books cited above were written by journalists; and indeed much of the content was derived from the columns the writers produced for magazines and newspapers. Instead of the magazine editor or publisher putting out large selections of material from the magazine, these books go from the writer for the magazine to the individually authored book.

As noted above, single-authored books from the early part of the century by Rundell, say, or Acton were normally addressed to the middle-class housewife. As her role shifted, and also as a result of many of the pressures of the edited collections discussed above, single-authored books diversified into works on the associated but *paid* work of cook or servant,[12] on the 'science' of domestic life (J. Buckmaster, *Buckmaster's Cookery*, 1874), on the attributes of fashion and status (C. Francatelli, *The*

Modern Cook, 1846), and on the social role the wife should take up (A. Soyer, *Book of Fashionable Life*). The single most urgent problem to be addressed by this substantial middle-class housewife was what to do with her time. If technology and commerce had radically changed her domestic responsibilities, the Industrial Revolution and urbanization created a vast group of people looking for work in domestic service to relieve this middle-class woman of any further need to work. In addition, where the husband's work may in earlier decades have been within reasonable distance of the domestic community, suddenly large numbers of urban working and middle-class men started travelling to work,[13] leaving the family at home with an increasingly private and isolated structure.

HOUSEHOLD LIFESTYLE

If the history of printed material answers some of the questions around the proliferation of small books in the latter part of the nineteenth century, it is the radical change in the lifestyle of the middle-class housewife and increasingly in the lifestyle of working-class and artisan housewives that holds the answers to several more. What I would now like to turn to are three interrelated issues: household management, the private family and the separation of the genders within the home. Against this background I shall focus on one particular specialized book, that addressed to an individual meal: not only did the books proliferate, but so also, as the other articles in this collection attest, did the meals.

Maria Rundell's *A New System of Domestic Economy*

(1806 and many later editions) is addressed to the middle-class housewife. While the text is organized largely by foodstuffs, very roughly in the order in which one might eat them at a dinner, the writer is not concerned with individual meals. She includes some notes of advice on having a 'well-regulated' dinner table in case the husband should bring home a visitor, and a few words on noonings and suppers 'for accidental visitors'; but the comments are in terms of the organization of eating around the traditional large dinner. Similarly Mrs Dalgairns's *The Practice of Cookery* (1829) is concerned with food within the general requirements of housekeeping, not with meals as such; and Esther Copley's *Cottage Comforts* (1825 and many later editions) intertwines household management with modes of cooking and preserving, as well as extensions into producing food for charitable purposes, as for the sick.

By 1845, the date of Eliza Acton's *Modern Cookery*, considerable attention is being given to ingredients. The introduction of foreign foodstuffs, the growing number of shops, and the increase in cases of food adulteration, may all have contributed to her focus on the detail of foodstuffs. Yet there is still little on meals themselves, even though the book is aimed at those with no experience of household management, the leisured children of the emergent bourgeoisie. In the 1855 revised edition Acton places more stress on well-prepared dinners, but is still mainly concerned with the purity of the foodstuffs and the organization of household economy around them. Webster's *Encyclopaedia of Domestic Economy* (1844) also speaks quite unselfconsciously to the middle-class housewife and describes a broad range of household economies;

but within this, although there is very little on the more mundane lunch, nooning, breakfast, or supper, there is advice on the social entertainments of desserts, routs and balls.

While Beeton's *Household Management* (1861) is derived from Webster, it is far more self-consciously middle class. It provides the specific metaphor of progress and civilization to the meal of dinner; and offers a special section on luncheon as a tide-you-over because urban working patterns make breakfast earlier and dinner later; suppers are described as less necessary in this domestic pattern. The whole of Beeton is arranged rather like a four-course dinner, with an emphasis on etiquette and upward mobility for the aspiring middle-class housewife. It is worth noting that from the middle of the nineteenth century certainly to at least the early twentieth, daughters of middle-class households were seen to be undereducated in household management, partly as a result of needing to appear leisured in order to maintain their family's social status. Both M. Careful's 'Julia' in *Household Hints* (1880) and O. Green's 'DS' or devoted spouse in *What to Have for Breakfast* (1905) suffer from this ignorance, as do many other examples.

Charles Francatelli explicitly addresses different classes of readers with different books. *The Modern Cook* (1846) is for the substantial middle-class housewife and is all about the organization of English, French and *à la Russe* dinners, between which fashionable competition is sweeping the country at the time. Yet his *Cook's Guide* (1862) which is addressed to the ordinary housewife, retains the more conventional two-course dinner alone, and provides brief additional information on breakfast and supper as domestic meals. Also dividing his books by class, Alexis Soyer first writes *The Modern Housewife* (1849) and then *A Shilling Cookery for the People* (1855). As with Francatelli, the later emergence of a book specifically concerned with daily domestic cookery, is probably tied to the change in publishing and printing that encouraged a broader readership in the 1850s and '60s.[14] What is significant is that the middle-class books treat the instructions about food preparation as if they are bound to a particular social gesture. Soyer's *Modern Housewife* starts with a dialogue about the importance of 'visiting', especially in the country. Following immediately from this is a discussion around the preparation of breakfasts and lunches as part of this social world; the book then goes on to focus on the preparation of dinner as the centrepiece to social entertainment.

Beeton of course roughly follows this pattern while transferring it to an urban setting. Many later substantial books such as *Cassell's Dictionary of Cookery* (1881), duplicate the focus on luncheon and breakfast dishes, with the 'dinner party' and its 'principles' as the heart of social entertainment within the home. Whereas Rundell assumes that dinners may be given to occasional guests and accidental visitors, Acton clearly notes the large numbers of rules for 'dinner'-giving and Beeton stresses that the 'dinner' is the middle-class housewife's contribution to upward social mobility. In 1889, A. Filippini's *The Table* says:

Nearly every family of means is in the habit of giving a few dinners to its friends during the year. As a matter of course, the members of the family are, in return, invited to 'dine' out. (p. 20)

And by the end of the century there are references to the madness of holding dinners more than four times a year; C.H. Senn's comments on the frequency of 'squalid' dinners indicate the chore that this social gesture had become. Simultaneously, breakfast, luncheon, picnics, teas and a variety of suppers – theatre, ball and rout – became meals invested with social gesture.

Significantly, most of the earlier specialized books are those on dining. In the 1840s it is clear that there were major changes in social dinner-serving to which many food writers for middle-class periodicals responded in a variety of partisan ways. *The Quarterly Review* of 1834–6 ran contributions from 'Walker's Original', who generated a range of post-Brillat-Savarin gastronomic literature often associated with men's clubs. George Vasey's *Illustrations of Eating* (1847), the anonymous *London at Table* (1851), J. Timb's *Hints for the Table* (1859) and W. Jerrold's *Epicure's Year Book* (1865 and later annual editions) are examples among many. Clubs, and to some extent pubs and taverns, provided the opportunity of eating away from home. This was often necessary during a long working day, but most of the gastronomic writers are treating dinner-going for men as a social activity. In several ways club culture can be seen as a mimicking of the illusion of aristocratic hospitality whose servants are plentiful and invisible. Timbs even refers to the need for circular tables 'to revive the chivalric glory of the round table' (p. 24). The clubs provided men with a home away from home where they were released from domestic responsibility essentially by paying a servant to provide the meal.

The elaboration of the domestic dinner into a social gesture may be seen at least partly as a response to this male-centred world. Certainly the books which focus on the housewife's preparation of such formal meals begin to be published in the 1860s–'70s, yet they also have their own social demands. An example is Mary Hooper's *Little Dinners* (1874), which *The Queen* notes as providing 'exactly what the young English wife wishes to know, and what the ordinary cookery-book does not teach her'. Hooper underlines the importance of mimicking higher-class gesture even in stringent economic circumstances (plate 13B). She says:

> All young housekeepers, and, indeed, not a few of the more experienced, know the difficulty of getting up little dinners for five or six persons without incurring too great an expense, or too severely taxing the powers of the cook. Such dishes as the time-honoured cod and oyster sauce, the haunch or saddle of mutton, always costly, are now quite beyond the reach of persons with small incomes, and it has become necessary for them to find less expensive substitutes, or to cease to dispense hospitality at all. (p. v)

At the same time Hooper has a nostalgia for the 'fashion of our grandmothers' time [when] . . . ladies would vie with each other in the art of preparing delicacies for the table' (p. xiii). She and a number of other writers in the 1870–90 period emphasize the importance of training young women in domestic economy so that they can maintain the appearance, if not the basis, of a substantial middle-class family (A. Bowman, *The New Cookery Book*, 1869, p. 589; J. Buckmaster, *Buckmaster's Cookery*, 1874, pp. 143 ff.; *Cassell's Dictionary of Cookery* 1881, p. xciv). Harriet de

Salis and Nancy Lake, both of whom write on dinners, in *The Art of Cookery* (1898) and *Menus Made Easy* (1884) respectively, as well as on other meals in the 1880s and '90s, are concerned with the cost and with keeping within moderate means, while maintaining social appearances. De Salis even publishes her books in different bindings: 1*s* 0*d* for those of moderate means and 1*s* 6*d* for those of substantial income. The education of the middle-class woman in domestic economy is focused on thrift, not frugality, thrift that enables the maintenance of fashionable status.

Mary Hooper is a writer who relates this social gesture intimately to the domestic life of the middle-class housewife. Her *Handbook for the Breakfast Table* (1873) describes the importance of a good breakfast to the 'busy city man' who swallows the poor breakfast in haste and then rushes off, often sustained only by a sandwich until dinner, frequently resulting in headaches and other ailments. The housewife in such a family is supported by servants, who are also part of the appearance of social status. Among her domestic responsibilities is to produce via the servants a good breakfast and a good dinner for her husband, and the occasional social dinner.[15] It is highly likely that this woman has few cooking skills herself, but she needs to know how to tell the servants to prepare meals, and so needs books that help her with this. Furthermore, socially oriented meals will often be 'à la mode' or 'recherché', fashionable, new and needing explanation: another reason for having a book about them. More interestingly, those people with servants have a lot less to do and are faced with the problem of 'filling in time'. Steel and Gardiner's *The Complete Indian Housekeeper and Cook* (1890) discusses the problem of eating too much and having too many meals, when there is too little to do. Even *Cassell's Shilling Cookery* (1888) notes that decoration of food takes time 'but there are a great many persons who would gladly employ their spare time, of which, they have plenty' (p. 324). Just so, there is the late-nineteenth-century emphasis on the need for the middle-class housewife to be able to produce *one* dish for herself, partly because it demonstrates competence and skill to her husband and servants, and partly because it gives her physical exercise (!) and something to do.

Although it is focused in a particular way, the picture drawn by these writers is of a group of women who no longer have active household work, whose duty is to the maintenance of domestic and social appearances, and whose lives are increasingly separated from men and isolated from one another. A. Hayward's *The Art of Dining* (1852 and new edition of 1883) notes that women never dine in public. Indeed, even if she has an expendable income, there are few places a woman can go in public with her husband, fewer with another woman, and even fewer on her own. In response, women elaborated on the social gesture of 'visiting' which came from the country house, and constructed a sophisticated set of domestic and social occasions in the home which were located around food.

Usually middle-class women ate at home, only joining their husbands for breakfast, and eating lunch, tea and occasionally supper rather than dinner. Major L. . . in *Breakfasts, Luncheons, and Ball Suppers* (1887) refers to lunch as 'the ladies' meal' (p. 26) and Mary Ronald's *Luncheons* (1902) notes that men are invited to lunch only on special occasions. Breakfasts move away from the 'light' meal of the 1850s (Philp, *Housewife's Reason Why*, 1857; Timb, *Hints for the Table*, 1859), and become highly elaborate. Book after book, from A. Kenney Herbert's *Fifty Breakfasts* (1894), M.L. Allen's *Breakfast Dishes for Every Morning of Three Months* (14th edn, 1892), H. Southgate's *Things a Lady Would Like to Know* (1881), Florence Jack's *Breakfast and Savoury Dishes* (1903), even the educational L.O.C.'s *Breakfast and Savoury Dishes* (1885), to C.H. Senn's *Ideal Breakfast Dishes, Savouries and Curries* (1910) and *Breakfast and Supper Dishes* (1898), talk about the boredom of the average breakfast table, the monotony of breakfast (M.L. Allen), of 'bacon and eggs' only occasionally relieved by 'eggs and bacon' (Kenney Herbert), and the need to make the meal interesting. The early commercial development of convenience food for breakfast underlines the importance of producing varied and interesting food for this meal, despite the constraints on time. Before these, O. Green tells us in *What to Have for Breakfast* (1905) women can produce 'a dainty, hygienic, satisfying breakfast' (p. 5) with forethought and 'persistent, if determined, cheerfulness'. These books also ally breakfast with savoury snacks that can be eaten by both husband and wife at supper.

It becomes apparent that the wife may only have expected to join the husband at dinner when it was a special occasion. A. Bowman's description of the dinner table implies that it is primarily for the man of the house, who expects to consume a fresh joint every day (p. 3). The social dinner, or dinner party, also becomes one of the few places where men and women who are not in the same family come together. Women are temporarily allowed to participate in a man's meal, and of course have to leave the table to the men at the end of it. M. Careful in *Household Hints* (1880) gives explicit instruction for a woman's participation in dinner when a (male) guest comes to eat:

> After dinner you sit awhile at the dessert and the wine passes, while conversation mingles with the pleasant smile. But when you find a little weariness pervading the scene, you rise and retire to the withdrawing room – this being of course always required when a friend is with you. (pp. 29–30)

Other mixed-gender social occasions such as the picnic, the ball-supper, the tennis party, also revolved around the preparation of meals specific to the occasion, often adopted because they satisfied the need to entertain but were in fact cheaper than formal dinners, yet still requiring books to instruct the housewife in the fashionable, and economic, presentation of them.

While the books on meals can give only a partial understanding of the way that women organized their lives, what is interesting is that the pattern of small and frequent meals in the home for women, and the focus on food as a social gesture, is found in books addressed to all classes of women by the 1890s. Even the textbooks used in ordinary schools such as Mary McNaughtan's *Lessons in Practical Cookery* (1895), not just those for middle-class women being trained in domestic economy such as those by Rose Owen Cole of the National Training School for Cookery (including her *Breakfast and Savoury Dishes*, 1885), were organized around these assumptions. As more families aspired to a bourgeois, middle-class lifestyle, the wives within those families were expected to adopt the private domestic world:

> Over the period from 1841 to 1914 the greatest change in women's occupations was the rising incidence of housewifery as the sole occupation for married women. In 1851, one in four married women (with husbands alive) was employed. By 1911, the figure was one in ten.[16]

The result is that an entire range of books addressed to audiences with quite different purposes – education, fashion and status, or domestic management – all begin to offer similar approaches to the structure of meals. The private housewife responded to social and domestic isolation with a series of gestures related to food. Her life revolved around a proliferation of small meals, a snack culture that places enormous emphasis on the significance of food preparation and presentation. Magazines and periodicals that carried the recipes, and the related published books, were essential to this development and went hand in hand with it, alongside the commercial, technical and technological changes of the late nineteenth century. Some of the questions arising from the initial starting point of the enormous explosion of specialized food books in the latter part of the nineteenth century may have been addressed. But we are now left with a further set: does this description of a social history relate to the food disorders of the twentieth-century western world?

FOUR

EVERYTHING STOPS FOR TEA

LAURA MASON

I like a nice cup of tea in the morning
For to start the day you see,
And at half past eleven
Well my idea of heaven
Is a nice cup of tea.
I like a nice cup of tea with my dinner,
And a nice cup of tea with my tea,
And when it's time for bed
There's a lot to be said
For a nice cup of tea.

Thus wrote A.P. Herbert in *Home and Beauty* of 1937, neatly summing up in verse one of the conundrums of British life: that tea is not only a drink, but also a meal. This has been so for about two hundred years. Matters are further complicated by the fact that tea meals have two entirely different forms, distinguished by the prefixes 'afternoon' and 'high'; and that both are usually called 'tea' with no further ado by the people who eat them. They know what they mean; but the two meals represent a wealth of social and regional differences, for those who eat dinner and then tea, as opposed to tea and then dinner, are likely to lead very different lives. This reflects a change in fashion with regard to the timing of dinner during the early nineteenth century, and much of the confusion can be traced back to that time. The difference between afternoon tea and high tea is intimately bound up with this confusion over the names, times and forms of meals, for high tea eaten after a midday dinner is likely to be a main meal and probably one taken in the provinces; and afternoon tea, eaten before an evening dinner, is a polite little snack. Only the British could squeeze so much meaning into a word three letters long.

William Ukers remarks that the general term 'tea' was used 'almost from the first to denote any occasion . . . where tea was served'; that tea, as a light repast served with the beverage tea as the evening meal, dates back only to the eighteenth century, and that '"High tea", or "meat tea", a meal with meats and other dishes served with tea, presumably was adopted after "tea" itself had become a regular meal; but when that was, English antiquarians have failed to discover'.[1]

The *Oxford English Dictionary* is not a great deal more informative; Fanny Kemble, a lady who obviously liked her tea, is credited with the first references to both high tea (in 1831) and afternoon tea. The latter, she remarked, she had first encountered in 1842 whilst staying at Belvoir Castle (seat of the Dukes of Rutland), and didn't believe it dated back much beyond that time. Ukers, however, says that it was Anna, wife of the seventh Duke of Bedford (1788–1861), who introduced afternoon tea with cakes as a custom; this was, she said, to counteract 'a sinking feeling' she got during the long hours between a light lunch and a fashionably late dinner at 8.00 p.m. The two types of tea might therefore be assumed to be quintessential Victorian meals. On closer examination it can be seen that, while afternoon tea depended much on the social customs of late eighteenth- and early nineteenth-century Britain, high tea bears a strong resemblance to seventeenth- and eighteenth-century dinners. The word 'high' may be a clue here, for, applied to eating and food, it carried a sense of richness during the seventeenth century. Possibly the expression high tea originally designated a more abundant meal than 'tea' alone; but that still doesn't tell us where or when this was first applied, although the fact that Fanny Kemble referred to it casually suggests that it was already well established. The expression 'meat tea' never seems to have become as common.

Mrs Beeton's *The Book of Household Management* (1880 edn) is a little more helpful, declaring:

There is Tea and Tea, the substantial family repast in the house of the early diner, and the afternoon cosy, chatty affairs that late diners have instituted. . . . The family tea-meal is very like that of breakfast, only that more cakes and knicknackery in the way of sweet eatables are provided. A 'High Tea' is where meat takes a more prominent part and signifies really, what is a tea-dinner. . . . The afternoon tea signifies little more than tea and bread-and-butter, and a few elegant trifles in the way of cake and fruit.[2]

From the names of the meals, the beverage tea might naturally be assumed to be the most important item on the table. This drink, first introduced to England in the seventeenth century, had become very fashionable and universally popular in the eighteenth century, partly due to the tea-gardens around London, to which the population resorted to drink tea, eat bread and butter and listen to music. Tea gradually became cheaper as more was imported and duty on it was reduced. By the early nineteenth century it had replaced home-brewed beer as a common day-to-day beverage of the labouring classes, much to the disgust of William Cobbett, who observed that it contained no nutriment and that the making of it wasted both time and fuel.[3] The rise of branded teas, such as Lipton's, in the nineteenth century established it firmly as a favourite English drink. However, both coffee and cocoa were sometimes served at high tea. Considerations such as foods, timing, location and social class are just as important as, if not more so than, the drink. The only item which the dictionary stipulates is essential to the definition of high tea is meat.

HIGH TEA AND ITS FARE

The modern idea of what a Victorian high tea would have consisted of contains elements of nostalgia for a simpler time, which include good plain cooking and a close family life, both ideals of the late nineteenth century. The plain cooking probably consisted largely of home baking; and the association of high tea with family life may well derive from the fact that in working-class homes it was dished up in the early evening, a time when the family usually had an opportunity to relax together. In upper-class homes, the children's evening meal would be tea in the nursery, not dinner with the adults. Nostalgia is also a feature of the best descriptions of high tea in literature from the nineteenth and twentieth centuries.

A very full description of the meal comes from J.B. Priestley's play *When We Are Married*, written in the 1930s, but reflecting social customs going back to the late nineteenth century. In the opening scene, Ruby, the 'slavey' or maid of all work, describes to a visitor what is being consumed at the 'do' in the dining room. 'Roast pork, stand pie, salmon and salad, trifle, two kinds of jellies, lemon-cheese tarts, jam tarts, swiss tarts, sponge cake, walnut cake, chocolate roll, and a pound cake kept from last Christmas' is only the beginning; the litany continues with white and brown bread, currant teacake, a bought curd tart and 'a lot o' cheese'; not to mention 'a little brown jug', the spirituous contents of which have to be elucidated for the visitor, who is not accustomed to putting rum in his tea.[4]

It is a good example of a really slap-up high tea menu. All the ingredients are there. Meat, essential to the definition, is the most important element, and is found in two forms: a roast of pork (which could be cold), and a stand pie. Then, as it appears that this is a really festive occasion, both fish (in the form of salmon) and cheese are involved. As well as all these delicacies, puddings are provided: the trifle, which was definitely for high days and holidays, and two jellies.

These items are supplemented by bread. No doubt this would have been sliced and buttered and laid out very nicely, perhaps on glass plates commemorating

Queen Victoria's Jubilee. Baking skills (probably those of someone in the household) are well represented by a good many cakes large and small, but the curd tart (a true Yorkshire speciality) was bought. Ruby omitted to mention that there would almost certainly be celery to eat with the cheese, and probably a good selection of pickles, such as red cabbage, beetroot, or piccalilli.

A final flourish is added with the 'little brown jug' of rum. Tea, as a drink, isn't mentioned until the contents of this are clarified; it is simply assumed to be there, implied by the context of the meal. The habit of adding rum or other spirits to tea has a venerable history, for in 1750 Dr Thomas Short wrote in his *Discourses upon Tea* of the 'too common pernicious Custom of drinking it with volatile Spirits, Drams etc'.[5] Milk and sugar would no doubt be provided; or maybe cream, which was sometimes preferred.

This substantial meal is awash with thoroughly traditional British food. Many of the dishes enumerated have their origins in much earlier times. Raised pies and jellies were known to medieval cooks, as were the spiced and fruited breads now so closely associated with tea-drinking that they are known as teacakes. Versions of trifle, pound cake, sponge cake, jam tart and curd tart are recognizable in seventeenth- and eighteenth-century recipes. The nineteenth century contributed to the repertoire yet more baked goods such as the swiss tarts, walnut cake and chocolate roll. It was in the provision of the large range of home-baked goods – cakes, pastries and breads, so important to both afternoon tea and high tea – that the British housekeeper really shone. Home baking was given a boost in the nineteenth century as the products of the new food-processing industries became cheaper and more readily available. Refined flour and sugar were two of the most important ingredients for baking, and both became cheaper and easy to obtain during the course of the century. Manufacturers advertised these goods heavily, especially the white flour, milled from cheap North American wheat by the newly invented roller mills, and finer and whiter than even the best, most carefully sifted flour available to cooks of previous centuries. Two other important contributions to the life of the home baker were made by nineteenth-century technology; these were baking powder, and the kitchen range. Baking powder, a product of the industrial chemist, came into use in the middle of the century. It was easier and less time-consuming for the cook to use than the traditional cake-raising agents of yeast and beaten egg. The cast-iron kitchen range with an integral oven, fired by coal, became commonplace in even relatively poor households by the mid-nineteenth century, and allowed a good deal more baking to be carried on at home.

Another important innovation which contributed to high tea was the preservation of food by canning. One is left to guess whether the salmon in this case is fresh or tinned, but my guess is the latter. Salmon was first canned in California in 1864; by the 1870s salmon-canning had spread to Columbia and Alaska, where it became an important industry. Tinned goods of all sorts had great cachet when they were first introduced to this country in the late nineteenth century (corned beef was an exception). Poorer households often didn't possess a tin opener, and the cans had to be taken to the grocer's for opening when the contents were needed. Tinned salmon was considered a real treat, a worthy dish to set before an honoured guest.

Two foods which Priestley doesn't mention, but which the members of one of the West Yorkshire Women's Institutes assure me were essential for high tea, were tinned peaches and seed cake. Tinned fruit must have been such a luxury in the days when everyone had to rely on seasonal domestic produce. Seed cake is another very traditional English cake, well known in the eighteenth and nineteenth centuries, although not always particularly appreciated. Mrs Gaskell, in her novel *Cranford*, notes an 'abundantly loaded tea tray' (in this case for an afternoon tea) containing a seed cake which was described as being reminiscent of scented soap.[6]

TEA MEALS IN THE VICTORIAN NOVEL

Great Victorian novelists also used descriptions of tea meals to evoke memories of bygone plenty in novels which were set in the past. Charlotte Brontë, in her novel *Shirley*, describes a scene in which three curates arrive unexpectedly one afternoon at a Yorkshire rectory, and are invited to tea:

Yorkshire people, in those days, took their tea round the table; sitting well into it, with their knees duly introduced under the mahogany. It was essential to have a multitude of plates of bread and butter, varied in sorts and plentiful in quantity: it was thought proper, too, that on the centre plate should stand a glass dish of marmalade; among the viands was expected to be found a small assortment of cheesecakes and tarts; if there was also a plate of thin slices of pink ham garnished with green parsley, so much the better.

Eliza, the Rector's cook, fortunately knew her business as provider: she had been put out of humour a little at first, when the invaders came so unexpectedly in such strength; but it appeared she regained her cheerfulness with action, for in due time the tea was spread forth in handsome style; and neither ham, tarts, nor marmalade were wanting among its accompaniments.[7]

Anyone familiar with high tea can recognize it in this description, but what is not clear is whether Charlotte Brontë, who was born in 1816, was writing from hearsay or from her memories of customs during her childhood in the 1820s, for *Shirley* is set against a background of the Luddite Riots in 1811–12.

A comparable description of tea is given by Dickens in *Barnaby Rudge*. It is produced by Mrs Varden for Dolly and Joseph Willet:

for whom the best service of real undoubted china, patterned with divers round-faced mandarins holding up broad umbrellas, was now displayed in all its glory; to tempt whose appetites a clear, transparent, juicy ham, garnished with cool green lettuce-leaves and fragrant cucumber, reposed upon a shady table, covered with a snow-white cloth; for whose delight, preserves and jams, crisp cakes and other pastry, short to eat, with cunning twists, and cottage loaves, and rolls of bread, both white and brown, were all set forth in great profusion.[8]

Barnaby Rudge, although published in the 1840s, was set in the London of some seventy years earlier, in

1775. The two quotes are almost contemporary in terms of publication date, and sound so similar that it's impossible to say whether they reflect habits of four to seven decades earlier, or whether both are more relevant to the 1840s. Brontë, at least, explicitly referred to her tea as a custom of the time she was writing about. What they do show clearly is that when these books were written, the concept of an elaborate tea involving meat, preserves and many baked goods was well established. Neither author saw fit to distinguish their teas with the prefix 'high', but in both cases undertones of generous hospitality and considerable abundance creep in. Finally, note the importance of ham, which represented the height of bourgeois gentility to the nineteenth-century poor, eventually giving rise to the funeral tea cliché of being 'buried with ham'.

There are many more examples of teas, both afternoon and high, in English literature. In many novels half the action appears to take place against a background of laden trays and an accompaniment of clinking china. It's a mark of how important tea, and the opportunity it provides for gossip, is to our social lives.

THE EVOLUTION OF HIGH TEA

How did high tea evolve from earlier meal patterns? To answer this, the timing, function and social context of the meal should all be examined. Timing is important: about four o'clock for afternoon tea, and between five and six o'clock for high tea. These times were dictated by those at which other meals were eaten by different social classes. In the eighteenth century tea was drunk both at breakfast and after a mid-afternoon dinner. Throughout the century, dinner got later, but the habit of afternoon tea-drinking seems to have stuck; whether or not the Duchess of Bedford really invented afternoon tea, or simply made fashionable a custom which was already established, is debatable. High tea was taken in the late afternoon or early evening, at about the time that people in the late eighteenth century had been accustomed to eat dinner.

As far as function and social context are concerned, afternoon tea was taken earlier because of the role it played as a 'filler', between the light nooning or luncheon and the late dinner fashionable amongst the late eighteenth- and early nineteenth-century gentry (Queen Victoria was said to dine as late as 8.00 p.m.). Compared to afternoon tea, high tea was an altogether more utilitarian meal, whose main function was serious eating: 'I'd rather keep Councillor Albert Parker for a week than a fortnight', remarks Priestley's 'slavey'.[9] Afternoon tea, on a physical level, provided some refreshment, but was also important socially, giving an opportunity to gossip and show off linen, silver and china; it fitted in, too, with the Victorian ritual of the afternoon visit. It was an adjunct to the other meals of the day, whereas high tea was a main meal for those accustomed to it. The function of the latter as a vehicle for gossip was largely incidental. One aspect which both meals did share was the way in which they could be elaborated into celebrations merely by adding a few more cups and saucers and a birthday cake; their timing made them especially suitable meals for celebrating children's birthdays, as various nineteenth-century paintings show.

1. A family at tea in the 1860s (Hulton Deutsch Collection)

2A. A dinner-table scene illustrating Victorian attitudes to class differences (*Punch*, 1872)

SAT UPON.

Hospitable Host. "Does any Gentleman say Pudden?"
Precise Guest. "No, Sir. No Gentleman says Pudden."

2B. Mealtime in a poor family's home in the 1850s (*Punch*, 1852)

3A. Londoners fetching their Christmas dinner from the baker's in 1848
(Drawing by John Leech, *Illustrated London News*, 1848)

3B. Dining Room at Langton, Family at Breakfast, *Mary Ellen Best*, *c.* 1834
(Private collection; photograph: Bridgeman Art Library)

4A. Breakfast table laid for eight persons (I. Beeton, *The Book of Household Management*, new edition, *c.* 1888)

4B. A country-house breakfast in the 1850s (*Punch*, 1852)

5A. After breakfast in the 1870s (*Punch*, 1877)

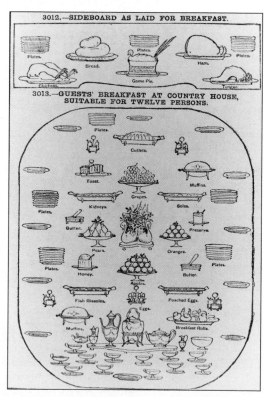

3012.—SIDEBOARD AS LAID FOR BREAKFAST.

Plates. Bread. Plates. Ham. Plates.

Chickens. Game Pie. Tongue.

3013.—GUESTS' BREAKFAST AT COUNTRY HOUSE, SUITABLE FOR TWELVE PERSONS.

Plates.

Cutlets.

Toast. Muffins.

Grapes.

Plates. Kidneys. Soles.

Butter. Preserve.

Pears. Oranges.

Plates. Honey. Butter. Plates.

Apples.

Fish Rissoles. Eggs. Poached Eggs.

Muffins. Breakfast Rolls.

5B. Plan of sideboard and guests' breakfast table (I. Beeton, *The Book of Household Management*, new edition, 1880)

6A. A pottery egg-cover for breakfast eggs
(J. Gouffé, *Royal Cookery Book*, 1868)

6B. Father and daughter at breakfast in the 1890s
(*Strand Magazine*, vol. 6, 1893)

7A. Breakfast and tea china. On the original plate the highly decorated items of china are coloured pink, blue or yellow (I. Beeton, *The Book of Household Management*, new edition, c. 1888)

7B. The curate's egg: 'Parts of it are excellent!' (*Punch*, 1895)

8A. Harvesters settle down to their bever
(Rural History Centre, University of Reading)

8B. A luncheon of cheese (W.H. Pyne, *Microcosm*, 1808)

9A. Queen Victoria with members of her family at the end of luncheon at Windsor Castle. The clock on the wall behind the queen shows half-past two (The Royal Archives

PLEASURES OF VEGETARIANISM.

"OH, GRACIOUS, MISS LEGUME! I FEAR I HAVE TASTED ANIMAL FOOD. I HAV EATEN A WHOLE EARWIG IN MY SALAD!"

9B. Vegetarians at lunch: a comment by a Punch artist on the newly popular vegetarian movement (Punch, 1852)

10A. Luncheon table laid for eight persons (I. Beeton, *The Book of Household Management*, new edition, *c*. 1888)

10B. The hazard of allowing a child of the house to attend a lunch party: the hostess's excuse for a 'poor lunch' due to her cook's influenza is followed by daughter's comment, 'Oh, Mummy, you always say that' (*Punch*, 1895)

11A. Dinner is served (Second frontispiece to *Beeton's Housewife's Treasury of Domestic Information*, 1880)

11B. Front cover of *The Quickest Guide to Breakfast, Dinner & Supper* ('Aunt Gertrude', *c*. 1880)

12A. Various fish garnished ready for serving (Plate from I. Beeton, *Everyday Cookery and Household Book*, 1891)

Dressed Crab

Oysters

Whitebait

Lobster

Brochet of Smelts

Red Mullet in cases

Salmon

Brill

Turbot

Whiting

Eels

Mackerel

Haddock

Cod

Trout

Soles

12B. Dinner *à la Russe* (Drawing by G. Dumaurier, *Punch*, 1876)

13A. Dining-room of the Sublime Society of Beef Steaks (W. Arnold, *The Life and Death of the Sublime Society of Beef Steaks*, 1871)

GENTEEL POVERTY DINING IN STATE.

13B. Punch provided this comment on those who 'mimic higher class gesture even in stringent economic circumstances' (*Punch*, 1867)

14A. Boating-party picnic, with plentiful liquid nourishment (Rural History Centre, University of Reading)

14B. Cookery school lesson (C.M. Buckton, *Food and Home Cookery*, 1879)

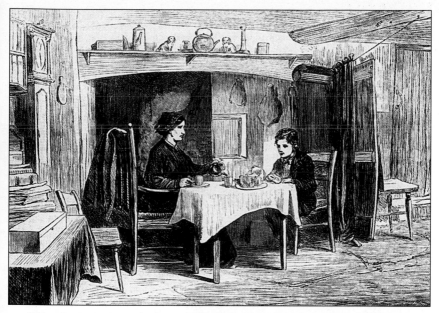

15A. Cottage tea at the home of Joseph Arch, the agricultural trade union
leader. Mrs Arch pours tea for her third son, Edward
(*Illustrated London News*, 1872)

15B. Tea in the nursery.
The head nurse tries to
dissuade Miss Mary from
stirring her tea with the
candle-snuffers (*Punch*,
1855)

16A. Assorted cakes, with a bride cake at centre in front and a christening cake decorated with a bassinet above it (I. Beeton, *The Book of Household Management*, c. 1888)

16B. *The Lord gave, and the Lord hath taken away*, Frank Holl, 1869. The funeral tea was, sadly, a frequent occasion in Victorian times (Guildhall Art Gallery, City of London; photograph: Bridgeman Art Library)

17A. *Baby's birthday*, by Frederick Daniel Hardy (1827–1911)
(Wolverhampton Art Gallery)

17B. Afternoon tea. Pictures of
the fashionable afternoon-tea
table with retractable wings also
appear in contemporary
editions of I. Beeton, *The Book
of Household Management*
(*Punch*, 1895)

18A. Union tea. Ladies from the Union Workhouse enjoy a celebratory tea out of doors, perhaps on the occasion of Queen Victoria's Diamond Jubilee (Blackett Collection, Rural History Centre, University of Reading)

18B. Tea table, 1906 (I. Beeton, *The Book of Household Management*, new edition, *c.* 1906)

19A. A first course for six, early eighteenth century (Drawing by Peter Brears)

19B. Christmas dinner (Drawing by R. Caldecott, in *Old Christmas from the Sketchbook of Washington Irving*, 1876)

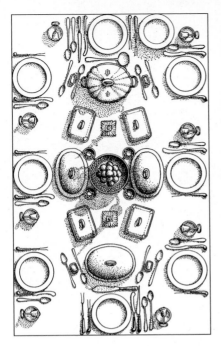

20A. The first course. The epergne stands in the middle of the table with a candlestick towards the top and bottom. The soup tureen, ladle, and soup plates are ready for use at the top of the table, while the fish awaits beneath its dish-cover at the bottom, ready to be served with the fish slice. Two side dishes, covered with dish-covers, flank the epergne, while four covered entrée dishes occupy the corners of this symmetrical arrangement. Note the tablespoons flanking the salt-cellar at each corner. Around the table each place is set with a hot dinner plate, a knife, fork, tablespoon for soup, and a wineglass in its cooler. The top and bottom places are also set with a carving knife and fork, and a gravy spoon, for serving the removes (Drawing by Peter Brears)

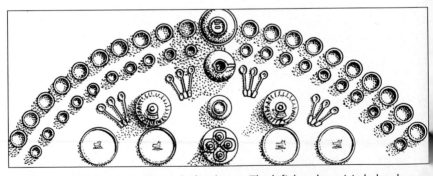

20B. The sideboard set out ready for dinner. The left-hand semicircle has large wineglasses on the outside and small wineglasses on the inside, while the right-hand semicircle has large rummers on the outside, and small liqueur glasses on the inside. Down the centre of the sideboard, in order from the back (top) to the front, are the lamp or candelabra, the water jug, the sugar basin, and the cruet stand. Decanters in their stands are arranged to each side, with a number of waiters along the front edge, ready to receive the glasses for services at the dining table (Drawing by Peter Brears)

21. At the dinner table, 1823 (Frontispiece to M. Radcliffe, *A Modern System of Domestic Economy*, 1823)

22A. Carving at table (F. Bishop, *The Illustrated London Cookery Book*, 1852)

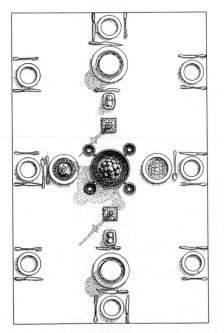

22B. The cheese course. Here the epergne and candlesticks are flanked by a dish of salad, and one of cucumber, with the appropriate cutlery, while cheeses stand both at the top and the bottom of the table, close to the butter dishes, containing butter cast into ornamental shapes using specially carved wooden moulds. Cheese plates, knives and forks are set before each person (Drawing by Peter Brears)

23A. The dessert course. After the cloth (or slips) has been removed, the epergne and candlesticks have been replaced, and the dessert course set out with the sugar bowl and the water jug standing close to the candlesticks. Each place has been set out with a dessert plate, knife, fork and spoon, and two glasses. Two decanters stand near the bottom of the table, where they may be un-stoppered and sent around by the host (Drawing by Peter Brears)

23B. *The Empty Cupboard*: a scene in a poor cottage in the centre of Sheffield (*Illustrated London News*, 1879)

24A. *Our Dining Room at York*, 1838, by Mary Ellen Best (See also plan 23B.)
(Private collection; photograph: Bridgeman Art Library)

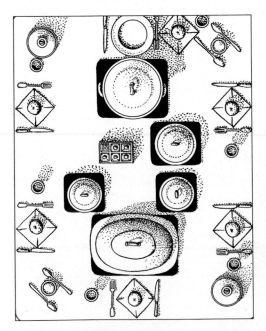

24B. The first course in Mary Ellen Best's dining-room at York in 1838. The soup tureen and soup plates are placed at the top of the table, with a covered dish at the bottom, and three covered tureens and a cruet stand in the middle. Decanters occupy one pair of diagonally opposite corners, with tablespoons and a salt-cellar at the others. Each place is set with a knife and fork flanking a dinner-bun placed on a square-folded napkin, and has a wineglass to the left-hand side (Drawing by Peter Brears)

25A. Dinner *à la Russe* (Drawing by G. Dumaurier, *Punch*, 1882)

25B. Round table laid for dinner *à la Russe* (F.U. Dubois, *Artistic Cookery*, 1870, (Guildhall Library, City of London)

26A. Epergne (Drawing by Peter Brears)

26B. Two Englishmen dining *à la Russe* in France. First Englishman: 'This is what they call à la Russe, isn't it?' Second Englishman: '"Allerouse" is it? Well there, I could a' sworn it warn't Beef or Mutton.' (*Punch*, 1863)

27A. The dining-room at Linley Sambourne House, now in the care of the Victorian Society (© RCHME Crown Copyright)

27B. Dinner party at Balnagown Castle, *c.* 1900. This photograph shows that it was possible to enjoy some informality at an *à la Russe dinner* (Tain District Museum (Scottish Ethnological Archive, Royal Museum of Scotland))

28. Glassware (I. Beeton, *The Book of Household Management*, new edition, c. 1888)

29A. The child who recognized the 'butler' as the family's greengrocer
(*Punch*, 1874)

29B. Rectangular table laid for modified diner *à la Russe* (J.H. Walsh, *A Manual of Domestic Economy*, 1890. By permission of the British Library)

30A. Soirée of the Vegetarian Society, 1851 (*Illustrated London News*, 1851)

30B. Supper for three in the 1890s (*Strand Magazine*, vol. 2, 1891)

31. Plan of supper table for ten to twelve persons (I. Beeton, *The Book of Household Management*, new edition, *c.* 1888)

32A. Two supper tables, with buffet behind (I. Beeton, *The Book of Household Management*, new edition, 1906)

32B. A working man's supper in 1871. The husband has lost his reason to grumble now he has won a working-day of nine hours. His wife suggests he should 'grumble for me, as I've done fourteen and ain't finished yet'
q(*Punch*, 1871)

Timing is not the only characteristic which high tea shares with the eighteenth-century dinner. The structure of the meal is also similar. The menus given at the back of eighteenth-century cookery books and in diaries[10] show that an eighteenth-century dinner consisted of a large number of dishes put on the table in two courses. Little distinction was made between sweet and savoury foods, so an apricot tart might share the table with a dish of green peas. Diners chose what they pleased from the foods available. This pattern is echoed by high tea. It is true that this meal was not usually divided into courses in the formal way that the dinner was; and it also involved many more baked items, which could be eaten with the fingers. Nevertheless, eaters 'invented' the courses for themselves, choosing from the selection available. Hot food or cold cuts and salad were eaten first, rather in the manner of an eighteenth-century remove, before progressing to toast, teacakes or crumpets and the numerous cakes. Afternoon tea was an altogether politer meal. The food which was served to accompany this was always very delicate, with the emphasis on thinly cut bread and butter, and a few delicate little sandwiches and cakes. Sandwiches were not usually served for high tea, although one might make a sandwich with the various items on the table.

To really confuse the issue, one could introduce the subject of supper, which appears to have been a meal similar in form to high tea, but taken at a later hour. Elaborate suppers were served during balls. The same types of dish were considered suitable for supper as for teas in the early nineteenth century. Meg Dods listed dishes suitable for a formal supper in her *Cook and Housewife's Manual*,[11] and they include the familiar list of cold cuts, ham, 'collared and potted things', pies, dressed fish, cakes, tarts, creams and so on. Mrs Gaskell observes in *Cranford* that shopkeepers 'gave comfortable suppers after the very early dinners of that day, not checked by the honourable Mrs D—'s precedent of a seven o'clock tea on the most elegant and economical principles, and a supperless turnout at nine', neatly illustrating social differences between her characters.[12]

Perhaps dinner and supper merely got reversed in their timing? It seems unlikely, although meals similar in all aspects to high tea are called 'supper' by some people even today. It is more probable that high tea represents a fossilized version of eighteenth-century dinner, reduced in scale and mostly served cold. The quantity and types of food eaten, the unstructured form, and the timing of high tea all support a close association with dinner as known in the seventeenth and eighteenth centuries.

Social class was also important to the definition of high tea. Afternoon tea was a meal generally consumed by those with plenty of leisure time; high tea was for those with work to do. J.B. Priestley's civic luminaries were self-made men, and they stuck with the habits of their younger days – although Priestley's text suggests that times were changing. The idea of high tea does not seem to have appealed to young Miss Holmes (niece of one of the main characters); and it appears to have been mildly amusing to her suitor, Gerald (Priestley implies he didn't come from Yorkshire). Tea, in the sense of a substantial high tea, really seems to have come to general notice in the second half of the nineteenth century, when it enjoyed a vogue amongst the Victorian upper middle class. This is probably the time when the real differentiation of 'tea' into two types, afternoon and high, started to be made, by a social class who were less familiar with tea as a main meal.

One reason why high tea may have become more popular with these people could have been that it was essentially a cold meal which could be prepared in advance and left ready for serving with very little help on the cook's afternoon off. Another may have been economy; for one of the editions of Mrs Beeton's *Book of Household Management* states that 'Tea, even when substantial, makes less demands on the resources of the household than breakfast, luncheon or dinner. Good housewives, with the necessary time at their disposal, contrive, even when other means are limited, to have a store of home-made jams, jellies and cakes at their disposal. When more plenteous meals are required, sandwiches, preserved and potted meat, offer a wide choice in this direction. Galantines, chaudfroid of chicken, simply dressed fish and nearly all breakfast and supper dishes are equally suitable for "High Tea".'[13]

High teas, or 'dining-room teas' as they were sometimes known, came to be regarded as rustic affairs by those who were accustomed to evening dinner. As late as 1939 Lady Troubridge wrote:

A large table is spread with a plain white cloth, and, set out with an entire loaf, farmhouse fashion, butter in an earthenware crock, and jam in its own pot, is a heartening sight, and guests invited to a meal of this kind invariably make a far larger tea than they would have in the drawing room. This is the tea of the week-end cottage, or the large family, and it should be kept very 'farmhouse' in details, with a big brown teapot, and not your favourite tea-set, but gaily patterned, thick tea-ware instead.

This, too is the correct way to serve 'high tea', and a dish of eggs or ham, or a tin of sardines on a plate, looks quite at home in this setting. Sizzling hot sausages in an earthenware dish, or scrambled eggs mixed with flaked haddock, are 'just right' foods to offer at the high, six o'clock tea.[14]

High tea is often strongly associated with provincial England, especially the north; this is reflected in the *OED* definition, where 'tea' as the name for a main meal is given as a northern usage, and the meal is deliberately used as a cliché of Yorkshire life by Priestley. The link between substantial teas and the north extends into Scotland, where evidently a large tea was well known early in the nineteenth century. F. Marian McNeill quotes some correspondence between two Scottish ladies at this time:

In the vera [sic] best houses, [writes Mrs Pringle from London to her friend, Miss Nancy Eydent, in Ayrshire] what I principally notised [sic] was, that the tea and coffee is not made by the lady of the house, but out of the room, and brought in without sugar or milk or servors [sic], everyone helping himself, and only plain, flimsy loaf bread and butter is served – no such thing as short-bread, seed-cake, bun, marmalet [sic] or jeely [sic] to be seen, which is an okonomical [sic] plan, and well worthy of adoption in ginteel [sic] families with narrow incomes, in Irvine or elsewhere.[15]

I am reliably informed that Scottish high teas are still quite an event, with particular hotels in various towns being well known for the quantity and quality of this meal. Apparently the two essentials (apart, presumably, from a pot of tea) are a cooked course, such as sausage and chips, followed by a cake-stand containing shortbread, scones and buns.

Why should the link with the north be so strong? Was the north more affluent? The quote from *Shirley* shows that elaborate teas were well known in Yorkshire from at least the first half of the nineteenth century, and were simply described as 'tea'. But Dickens, writing in London, expected his readers to be equally familiar with the concept. Perhaps some public relations work was involved: for one great popularizer of high tea in the late nineteenth century was Yorkshireman Joseph Wright, compiler of *The English Dialect Dictionary*, whose Sunday teas were famous in Oxford around the beginning of the twentieth century.[16] High tea also has a persistent association with the countryside. The poets of the Romantic movement in the early nineteenth century popularized country areas such as the Lake District, and railways, bicycles and a vogue for walking holidays encouraged people from towns to visit areas such as the West Country and the Yorkshire Dales. Peter Brears remarks that the ham and egg teas served at Dick Hudson's, a pub above Shipley on the edge of Ilkley moor, were famous; as were those at the British Temperance Tea Rooms in Eldwick.[17] Possibly the more conservative rural areas preserved customs which went out of fashion in the cities, including an early evening main meal of many different dishes, such as had been known among the gentry in the mid-eighteenth century.

Finally, during the nineteenth century, other factors which helped to popularize tea were its use by the temperance movement, who held 'tea meetings' as a means both of providing an audience for renouncing sinners, and of raising money; and use of tea as a refreshment on church and chapel outings, such as a walk described in *Shirley*[18] where a church tea was provided for the parish children, consisting of large currant buns and hot well-sweetened tea. Then there was the rise of the café. The popularity of tea-gardens had declined during the nineteenth century, but in the 1880s tea-rooms began opening as places of refreshment in the cities; some well-known chains were the ABC (this stood for the Aerated Bread Company), Lyons, and the Kardomah. Tea, hot meals, cakes, bread and pastries were all available in these places. They continued to be popular well beyond the end of the nineteenth century, and also provided venues for 'tango teas' during the 1920s. Tea, or high tea, remained popular as an evening meal through the Second World War and into the 1950s when a survey found that over 60 per cent of adults called their evening meal 'high tea'.[19]

The evidence seems to show that high tea and afternoon tea are two completely different meals. Although afternoon tea and high tea are both taken in the late afternoon, high tea has a much wider range of foods associated with it and is clearly intended to be a main meal. The fact that both meals are called 'tea' suggests a relatively recent origin, but high tea preserves the time and many of the characteristics of the seventeenth- and eighteenth-century dinner, fossilized as a phenomenon amongst the less wealthy and in the provinces. The fashionable and popular eighteenth-century drink, tea, has been grafted onto this meal, partly encouraged by the temperance movement, who looked with disfavour on the traditional English drinks of claret or beer. Afternoon tea, while it had older precedents in the little collations and light refreshments served in previous centuries, occupied a new niche, with a new format. I think it probable that it was only when tea as a main meal was adopted by the upper classes and the new 'tea-rooms' that the name 'high tea' really became common currency; since in areas where high-tea types of meal were traditional, they were simply called tea with no further ado. The quote from Brontë shows that this was true, in the north, as one might expect. That from Dickens suggests that even in London, an elaborate meal was sometimes simply known as tea. Perhaps the rise of high tea in the mid-Victorian period should be viewed as the gentrification of a meal laid aside by fashion in the late eighteenth and early nineteenth centuries, an unusual example of upward osmosis of a social custom.

FIVE

À LA FRANÇAISE: THE WANING OF A LONG DINING TRADITION

PETER BREARS

When Queen Victoria came to the throne, dinner was served to middle- and upper-class families in Britain in a manner which was already the product of centuries of continuity and change, for each succeeding generation had modified the practices of its predecessors to suit its evolving needs. In the sixteenth century most large households still dined in an essentially medieval manner around 10.00 a.m. each day. The master, mistress and chief guests usually sat behind a long table in their great chamber or dining parlour as two courses were carefully set out in turn before them. Service was provided from the front of the table by a specialist team of butler, panter, carver, sewer, etc. which formed an essential part of the establishment. Diners of slightly lower status might be seated at a second table in the same room, with appropriately lower standards of food and service, while the remainder of the household dined communally in the hall.[1]

The seventeenth century saw considerable changes occur in the dining room, as the extensive old-fashioned households with their wealth of ceremonial officers were reduced to much more compact and economical units. Now the family and guests tended to sit around a single table of rectangular or oval form in the middle of the room, although the second table continued in use in the provinces through into the succeeding century. Service was now provided by a butler and a few servants, who placed the first of the two courses on the table around 1.00 p.m., then acted as waiters through the remainder of the meal.[2] Other significant changes at this period included the gradual introduction of the fork, which replaced the use of the thumb and first two fingers of the left hand when dining, and the proliferation of printed cookery books which provided lists of dishes for each course, together with instructions as to where they were to be placed on the table.

As we enter the eighteenth century our knowledge of the food and customs associated with dining is greatly increased by the appearance of more detailed cookery books, and in due course by volumes such as Jonathan Swift's *Directions to Servants* of 1745 and John Trusler's *Honours of the Table* of 1788. As the latter stated:

> Of all the grateful accomplishments, and of every branch of polite education, it has been long admitted that a gentleman and a lady never shew themselves to more advantage, than in acquitting themselves well in the honours of the table; that is to say, in serving their guests and treating

their friends agreeable to their rank and situation in life.[3]

To do this, new dining rooms were constructed to the highest standards of design and elegance. Large rectangular tables and suites of dining chairs of polished hardwood occupied the central space, with a sideboard and a side-table against the walls to hold the equipment and other items required during the meal. The table was covered with a fine damask linen cloth as in previous centuries, but instead of the simple dishes, salt-cellars and saucers of earlier times, a whole range of new tablewares now began to appear. Usually made of silver, they included cruet frames and ornate epergnes from around 1715 (plate 26A); covered entrée dishes and tureens from the 1720s; and fish-slices and asparagus tongs from the 1740s. Saucers, originally small rimmed bowls had evolved into double-ended sauceboats by 1715, single-ended forms coming in around 1725, and sauce tureens around 1765. Instead of being laid with their prongs and bowls facing downwards, forks and spoons were now being laid with them facing upwards, in the modern manner, which meant that the curvature of their ends became reversed. In order to keep the dishes warm on their way from the kitchen to the table, they were covered with large domed dish-covers, while at the table were cross-shaped stands, each incorporating a spirit stove, to maintain their heat throughout each course.[4]

When all this equipment had been put in place, and the first course laid on the table, a servant informed the company waiting in a nearby room that dinner was served. This usually took place between 3.00 and 5.00 p.m.[5] Then the mistress of the house requests the lady first in rank, in company, to show the way to the rest and walk first into the [dining] room where the table is served; she then asks the second in precedence to follow, and after all the ladies are passed, she brings up the rear herself. The master of the house does the same with the gentlemen.

When they enter the dining-room each takes his place in the same order; the mistress of the table sits at the upper-end, those of superior rank next to her, right and left, those next in rank following, then the gentlemen, and the master at the lower end.

This meant that the sexes were segregated to their respective ends of the table, those of highest rank being seated furthest from the centre. In the 1780s, however, this custom began to give way to one which we find much more recognizable today, with

A gentleman and a lady sitting alternatively round the table, and this, for the better convenience of a lady's being attended to and served by the gentleman next her. But not withstanding this promiscuous seating, the ladies, whether above or below, are to be served in order, according to their rank or age, and after them the gentlemen, in the same manner.

After grace, the mistress told her guests either that they 'saw their dinner', meaning that no further dishes would be appearing, or that there would be 'removes' and what they would be. The remove was described by Dr Johnson in his great *Dictionary* of 1773 as 'a dish to be changed while the rest of the course remains'. In practice, it meant that the mistress would serve the soup, probably her husband would then serve the fish, after which these dishes were removed by two more substantial dishes, such as roast or boiled meat, etc. The mistress would then carve one remove, and ask the master, or whoever was sitting at the bottom end, to carve the other, while the servants proceeded to remove the covers of all the remaining dishes on the table. During this operation

> As eating a great deal is deemed indelicate in a lady, (for her character should be rather divine than sensual) it will be ill-manners to help her to a large slice of meat at once, or fill her plate too full. When you have served her with meat, she should be asked what kind of vegetables she likes; the gentleman sitting next the dish that holds those vegetables, should be requested to help her.[6]

While the gentlemen were helping the ladies, and then themselves, to whatever they wanted from this first course, the servants provided assistance by handing plates, bread, condiments and glasses of wine, beer, ale, etc. as required. Any diner who wished to move on from one food to another would slip the handles of the knife and fork into the plate, so that a servant would know that he should bring a fresh knife, fork and plate from the sideboard, and put it in place of those which had just been used.

When the first course had been finished, it was taken away and replaced by the second course, which usually lacked any removes. After this had been served, and the diners had finished eating, all the tableware was carried off, and a glass finger-bowl half-full of water placed before each guest so that they could rinse their fingers. This operation being completed, the finger-bowls and the table-cloth were removed, any marks were rubbed off the table, and the dessert course was set in place. When this had been finished and cleared, and two or three glasses of wine had been taken, the mistress rose, giving the ladies their lead. The gentlemen rose too, the nearest moving to the door to hold it ajar until the ladies had withdrawn, after which the gentlemen got down to some serious drinking, before rejoining the ladies later in the evening.

Having briefly outlined the development of dining during the seventeenth and eighteenth centuries, we will now follow the process of preparing and serving dinner during the early years of Queen Victoria's reign.[7]

The butler's first task was to decant the wine, using the left hand and both feet to hold the bottle firmly down on the floor while manipulating a corkscrew in the right hand to draw the cork, thus leaving the dregs undisturbed. Once the wine had been poured into the decanter through a cambric-lined wine-strainer, an engraved silver or handwritten paper label was immediately slipped around the neck of the decanter, to ensure that no mistakes were made when serving different wines of similar colour. The wine was then left in some secure place of appropriate temperature until required.

Then, when he had obtained from the cook all details of the dishes to be served, a bill of fare was drawn up, setting out how they were to be arranged on the table at each course. Special attention was paid to the particular requirements of the family. Some preferred to have the sauces and vegetables placed on the table, for example, while others had them handed round by servants.

LAYING THE TABLE

Most households still retained the long rectangular form of dining table of earlier centuries, since it made the most economical use of the available space, and could be easily extended to accommodate larger numbers of guests by the simple addition of extra leaves. In the 1830s, however, circular dining tables began to revive the chivalric concept of King Arthur's 'Round Table', a very expensive version being invented which expanded from its centre. There is one at Devonshire House of immense size. For these, special circular damask table-cloths were manufactured at considerable cost; setting the loom alone cost some £70.[8] Since very few families chose to make such a large investment, the rectangular table has retained its popularity through to the present day.

Having been dusted, the table was first covered with a thick cloth of green or red baize, which protected the polished surface, and improved the appearance of the completed setting. Now the glazed damask linen table-cloth was taken from the press, where it had been screwed down flat since breakfast-time, and was spread across the table. The hem confirmed which was the upper surface, while both the creases and the design established the centre-line for the middle of the table. If motifs of crests, coats of arms, flower baskets, etc., were woven into the cloth, they had to be positioned so as to be seen correctly when viewed from the foot of the table, the bottom of a basket being towards the bottom of the table, for example. On large tables, where it was more convenient to leave the cloth on the table for dessert, additional lengths of cloth called 'slips' were laid around the sides and ends, where they would receive most of the soiling which might occur during the course of the dinner. The first pieces to be set on the table were the epergnes, the plateau, the centrepiece and perhaps, from around 1830, displays of flowers along with the candelabra. Where used, mats were then put ready to receive the dishes, and a napkin, ornately folded both to display the family's crest, and to contain a bread roll, was placed before each chair. If rolls were not used, the bread was cut in pieces not less than an inch and a half (4 cm) in thickness.[9] The cutlery, salt-cellars, carvers, soup ladle, and gravy spoons were then carefully arranged, as in the first course diagram (plate 20A), together with water bottles and glasses, and wine decanters. Should glass coolers be used, they were two-thirds filled up with spring water, and the wineglasses turned upside-down within them.

If there were to be a number of changes of plates and cutlery, an extensive supply of additional tableware had also to be made ready in the dining room, perhaps as many as six large plates for each person, with pudding and cheese plates, and as many knives and forks. Three wineglasses and two rummers each were also required, with spares on hand in case of breakages.

The Sideboard

The sideboard, an impressive piece of furniture, usually of mahogany, may have stood along one of the side walls in the dining room, or at one end, if the room was long and narrow. Its principal purpose was to hold the wineglasses, drinks, cruet and sugar basin, set out as in the diagram (plate 20B), any open space being decorated with a few spare silver spoons, since their bright polished surface showed off the glassware to the best advantage.

The sideboard also accommodated jugs of beer, spring water and toast-and-water in a tray or cellaret, or on a knife-cloth. Here too were a plate-basket for the dirty plates; boxes and trays for the dirty knives, forks and spoons, where they could be kept separate to prevent scratching; and a small tray lined with a knife-cloth for removing the carving knife and fork from the dishes on the table after use.

The Side-table

Standing against the wall opposite the sideboard, the side-table held the cold plates, cheese plates and dessert plates, the salad, vegetables and cold meat, the steel knives and forks, and the silver knives and forks. Each dessert plate was covered with a doyley, on which stood a finger-glass of water, with a knife to the right, and a spoon and fork to the left, ready for placing before each diner after the table-cloth had been removed. As with the sideboard, every item standing on the side-table was arranged in a neat, attractive and symmetrical pattern.

PREPARING FOR DINNER

All the primary preparations being made, the half-hour before the dinner was actually served was occupied in lighting the lamps and candles both in the dining room and along the passageways leading from the kitchen. The beer, ginger-beer, porter, soda-water and spring water were brought in, the trays were taken to the kitchen, and the tray-stands put in their proper places. If there was a fire in the dining room, the plates were stacked in a plate-warmer, an elegant tinplate cupboard with an open back, which was placed before the fire-bars so that the plates could be thoroughly heated. Alternatively, they could be heated in the kitchen, and carried up just before dinner was served.

If any time was left, the cook could be helped to dish up the first course, a process which usually took around half an hour. The laden dishes were then carried up to the dining room on trays, while the soup tureens were carried up by hand, to ensure their safety. Each dish was carefully placed on the table in an exactly symmetrical pattern, which was quickly checked by sighting down its centre-line. This was very important, for the depressions left on the table-cloth by these first-course dishes acted as a guide for placing all the subsequent courses.

The position of the dishes was also determined by the bill of fare, particularly with regard to the top and bottom dishes. Here there was scope for considerable variety. If one soup was being served, it occupied the bottom of the table, with a roast at the top; if there were two soups, they might occupy both the top and the bottom, or, if fish occupied these places, the soups could be placed at each side of the table. If soup was not served, then it was usual for fish to occupy the bottom, again with a roast at the top.[10]

It was also important to ensure that each dish which had to be carved was placed in the most convenient position for the carver. Fish, hare, rabbits and roast pigs had their heads to his left, while most birds had theirs to the right, although turkey, goose and duck might have their heads to the left so that the carver could easily get at the stuffing. Hams, legs of mutton and haunches of venison had their shanks to the left, each other joint having its own particular position. If the meat-dish had a well at one end to collect the gravy and juices, this was placed at the right, so that the carver could easily serve its contents with a spoon. Once the dinner was on the table, the hot dinner-plates were set before each place; and the soup plates were put close to the tureen, a little to the left of the person who was to serve it.

SEATING

Having been summoned by either a bell or a gong, the guests gathered in a reception room close to the dining room. Here their hosts made appropriate conversation and introductions for about a quarter of an hour before the manservant approached and announced, 'Dinner is served, sir.' He then opened the dining room door, and took up his position outside it until all the company had entered.

The host took in the lady present of highest rank, and the gentleman of highest rank took in the hostess, each gentleman offering his right arm to the lady he escorted and, as they approached the table, he might draw out the lady's chair, if this was not already done by a servant. Usually the mistress occupied the chair at the head of the table, and the master that at the bottom, but if the company was large they could sit in the middle, so that they might concentrate on entertaining their guests, and be relieved of the duties of carving, etc.[11] They might direct their guests to their chosen places around the table, but this task could be organized much more efficiently by placing a small label bearing the name of each person within their respective plate.

SERVING DINNER

Once everyone was seated, a servant removed the cover off the soup. In this action, he should not emulate Mr Muleygrub's stiff-necked boy who 'gave the steam-degrimed cover a flourish in the air, and favoured his master's bald head with a hot shower-bath'. Instead, he should use his right hand, if on the right side, or his left hand, if on the left side, to quickly turn the cover upside down, so that the condensation would not drop on to the cloth. As the soup was served, a servant would hold each plate in turn on a level with, or slightly below, the rim of the tureen. To do this, he used his left hand, his thumb being placed on the rim, with his first two fingers crooked beneath it, pressing against the bowl of the plate, and his third and fourth fingers tucked neatly into his palm. Once the mistress had filled the soup plate, he then handed it to a guest, serving to the left side, until all those who wanted soup had been served. The order in which the diners were served was of the greatest importance. It was customary for those of first rank to be served first, dukes taking precedence over earls, for example, or baronets before gentlemen; those of equal rank were then served according to seniority of age, but with guests taking precedence over hosts. The rules of precedency were thus extremely complex, and it was most helpful if the lady or gentleman doing the serving could indicate to the servant where he was to carry each particular plate.

A similar procedure was followed for the fish, which the master, if acting as carver, served with silver fish-servers, since steel imparted an unpleasant flavour to this dish. If fried fish was being offered, it was usually divided into portions in the kitchen, for it was more easily served in this way. A servant might hand sliced cucumbers to the diners at this time, a silver fork and spoon being placed in the dish so that they could help themselves.

If any of the diners called for beer, water, wine, etc., during the course of dinner, a servant took one of the appropriate stemmed glasses, carefully holding the stem between the thumb and index finger of the left hand, with the second finger pressing upwards beneath the base, to give added stability. Using the right hand, he filled the glass about three-quarters full, and placed it on a small tray or waiter, close to one edge, so that, if necessary, the thumb could be used to keep it steady. Holding the waiter in the left hand, the servant then walked from the sideboard to the left-hand side of the diner, leaning forward so that the diner could take the glass with ease, and consume the drink. When the glass had been drained, the servant, who had been waiting behind the diner, lifted it with his right hand on to the waiter in his left, and carried it back to the sideboard, placing it where it could be used again if the same person required the same kind of liquor. If a different liquor was called for, then a clean glass was always used.

Once the soup and fish had been eaten, a servant took the soup ladle and fish knife with his right hand, placed them carefully on to a clean knife-cloth on a small tray held in the left hand, and cleared them from the table. At the same time, the plates might be changed, the soiled plate containing the soiled cutlery being removed with the right hand, while a clean plate containing clean cutlery was put in its place with the left. The soiled plates were then gently stacked in a plate basket, while the soiled cutlery was separated, knives from forks, etc., and placed in separate trays, so that there was a minimum of scratching.

The soup tureen and fish dish were then cleared from the table, their places being taken by the removes, if these were being served. If a single soup had been served, it would be removed by fish, while if two soups had been served, they would be removed by fish and a roast. Once the removes were on the table, all the dishes were uncovered, and the carver, usually the host, began his work. As Meg Dods stated:

Carving has long been esteemed one of the minor arts of polite life – a test at first sight of the breeding of men, as its dextrous and graceful performance is presumed to mark a person trained in good fashion. 'To dance in hall and carve at board' are classed together, by no mean authority in the list of a young gentleman's accomplishments; and Chesterfield, the great modern teacher of polished life, has made this qualification an object of his pupil's particular study. . . . To carve quickly and neatly requires a good deal of practice, as well as vigilant observation of those who perform the office well.

To cut warm joints fairly and smoothly, in slices neither too thick, nor finically thin, is all that is required of the carver of a plain joint, whether boiled or roasted. For this purpose he must be provided with a knife of suitable size, having a good edge; and it will greatly facilitate his operations if the cook has previously taken care that the bones in all carcase-joints are properly divided. It is impossible for the most dextrous carver to proceed with ease or comfort if this is neglected. In carving game or poultry for a large party, where many look for a share of the same delicacy, what is called 'making wings' must be avoided; the first helpings should be cut long way, and not made too large.[12]

Dr Kitchiner stressed that the distribution of the dainties should be undertaken by the master and the mistress, this being one of their pleasantest duties. At no time should the carving be left in the hands of a 'Chop-house Cormorant', one of those gentlemen who were the terror of good housewives from their practice of unmercifully mangling the joints in order to obtain their particular delicacy.[13] In contrast, the elegant carver always left the joint looking as presentable as possible, sometimes by rearranging the garnishing over it or, in the case of fish, by folding it beneath part of the napkin on which it was served.[14]

As the carver began his work, a servant standing a little behind him on his left held each plate in turn level with the rim of the meat dish to receive the slices.

Usually the servant used his left hand to hold the plate, but if the meat dish had no well to hold the gravy, he held the plate in his right hand, and used his left to raise his end of the meat dish, so that the carver could spoon up the gravy from the right. If any of the diners wishes to have cold meat, one of the servants would carve it from the joints set out on the side-table.

The plates of meat were then handed round by the servants, the vegetables and sauces being similarly handed round, always serving from the diner's left. Plates and cutlery were changed whenever a diner proceeded from one dish to another, a need indicated by placing the knife and fork in parallel position across the plate.

When the company appeared to have finished the first course, the master or mistress gave the signal for it to be removed. Starting at the bottom of the table, a servant proceeded up the left side, carefully lifting the carving knives, forks and spoons into a small knife-tray lined with a knife-cloth. Then, repeating the same route, he first removed the bottom dish, then the left-hand side-dishes, the top dish, and the right-hand dishes. For the large top and bottom dishes, he stood sideways to the table, to the left of the carver, leant forwards, and used both hands to raise them clear of the glasses, etc. In contrast, the smaller and lighter side-dishes were simply lifted off with one hand. They were then placed on trays and carried back to the kitchen.

Here the second-course dishes were arranged on the tray, if possible in the same manner as they were to appear on the table. Alternatively a copy of the second-course bill of fare was placed either on the tray or on the sideboard, where it could be used as a guide for setting the dishes in place on the dining table. A servant then removed the dish-covers, and the second course was served and removed in exactly the same way as the first.

For the third course, each diner's soiled dinner plate, knife and fork were changed for a cheese plate containing a small knife and, if there was a salad, a fork too (plate 22B). The third-course dishes were then put in place, usually with a cheese and cheese knives at the top and bottom, butter and butter knife in the middle, a salad with a spoon and fork to one side, and the sliced cucumber with a spoon to the other. While the company were eating their cheese, the servants removed all the unused cutlery from the table, along with the glass-coolers and wineglasses, since only porter or ale were normally drunk with this course.

When the third course was finished, every item was removed from the table, commencing with the cheese. Any pieces of bread were taken off, using either a table-brush, or a spoon and plate, and the crumbs cleared with a clean glass-cloth and plate. The finger-glasses were then put round, one for each person, to allow the diners to rinse their fingers and perhaps wipe their lips with a moistened corner of their napkin. As soon as this process had been completed, either the slips were removed, if the table-cloth was to be left in place, or the linen and baize cloths were removed together, and any dampness wiped off the polished surface of the table.

Once the dessert had been set in place, as in the dessert course diagram (plates 24A and 24B), a dessert plate and two wineglasses were placed before each person, after which the servants handed round the ices and the dessert wines. They then quickly, quietly and efficiently removed from the dining room every item which was not in use, except for the cruet stand and the clean glasses, plates and cutlery on the side-table. They then left the company to themselves, and began to wash and clean all the tableware and return it to its place in the pantry ready for use on some future occasion.

On the conclusion of dessert, the ladies retired to the drawing room to take tea or coffee; and the gentlemen remained to drink their wine, and sometimes took their coffee in the dining room before rejoining the ladies. Once the company had left the dining room, the butler immediately entered the room, put away the wine, and locked the door behind him until he had sufficient time to complete his work there. If this precaution was not taken, the servants were apt to strip the table of its remaining fruit and wine, theft of this kind leading to a breakdown in the discipline of the household.

This very full description of an early Victorian dinner *à la Française* demonstrates just how complicated this method of service could be in a fashionable household. Clearly it was beyond the means of many middle-class families, but they too followed the same sequence of courses. Perhaps the best evidence of this is provided by the finely detailed watercolour of *Our Dining Room at York* painted by Mary Ellen Best in 1838, which shows the first course on the table, just ready to be served (plates 23B and 24A).[15]

Here the tableware appears to be an attractive blue transfer-printed earthenware or ironstone china, a huge round soup tureen standing at the top of the table, a meat dish with a metal cover at the bottom, with three tureens placed two and one at the sides, and a cruet stand taking the place of the fourth tureen. Each piece is placed on a rectangular black-japanned mat in order to prevent any heat or moisture damage to the cloth-covered dining table. A stack of soup plates stands in front of the top chair, ready to be filled and passed around the table, while at diagonally opposite corners of the table stand a pair of decanters, and a salt-cellar between a pair of tablespoons lying with their bowls facing downwards. Before each chair, a round dinner-bun stands on a square folded napkin, between a knife and a fork, with a wineglass to the left-hand side. Presumably the tablespoons with which the soup was eaten are still to be set on the table. At any moment now the diners will enter, sit at their places, take their soup, and perhaps proceed on to the fish, or a roast concealed beneath the dish-cover, then a remove, or removes, before moving on to the second course.

The major problems with service of this type were: first, that it was difficult to keep food warm throughout single courses which included soup, fish, the carving of removes and the passing of vegetables, etc.; second, that the handing of dishes from the central area of the table either by diners or by servants was a troublesome affair; and third, that the process of dining *à la Française* brought frequent interruptions to the flow of conversation around the company. The time taken, and the trouble caused, by carving at the table were a constant cause of complaint. Take, for example, the following case:

An accomplished gentleman, when carving a tough goose, had the misfortune to send it entirely out of the dish, and into the lap of the lady next to him; on which, he very coolly looked her full in the face, and with admirable gravity and calmness, said – 'Madam, I will thank you for that goose.'[16]

The comment was also made that polite folk wasted as much time in making civil faces, etc., when carving for even a single guest, as it would take a dextrous carver to carve for six.[17]

The solutions were quite obvious. 'It would save a great deal of Time, etc., if Poultry, especially large Turkeys and Geese, were sent to table ready cut up', wrote Dr Kitchiner in 1822, while in 1829 Meg Dods hoped 'to see the day when all large troublesome dishes will be taken to the side-table, and carved by a maître d'hotel, or whoever waits on the company, as is now the general practice of France, Germany and Russia'.[18] Within a few years cookery writers were able to inform the public that this change was then taking place, and Isabella Beeton explained how for

Dinners à la Russe, the dishes are cut up on a sideboard, and handed round to the guests, and each dish may be considered a course. The table for a dinner à la Russe should be laid with flowers and plants in fancy flowerpots down the middle, together with some of the dessert dishes. A menu or bill of fare should be laid by the side of each guest.[19]

Mrs Beeton's *Book of Household Management* of 1861 gives just two examples of this new form of service, in contrast to eighty-one for à la Française, which shows how strong the old tradition was at this time. Instead of the former three courses, however, there are now five, as may be seen in her bill of fare for eight in January.[20]

EATING WITH THE VICTORIANS

First Course

Mulligatawny Soup

Brill and Shrimp Sauce   Fried Whitings

Entrées

Fricasseed Chicken   Pork Cutlets with Tomato Sauce

Second Course

Haunch of Mutton   Boiled Turkey with Celery Sauce

Boiled Tongue, garnished with Brussels Sprouts

Third Course

Roast Pheasants

Meringues à la Crème   Compote of Apples   Orange Jelly

Cheesecakes   Soufflé of Rice

Dessert and Ices

I. Beeton, *The Book of Household Management* (1861), p. 911

Already *à la Française* was half-way to becoming *à la Russe*. It only required the first course to be finally divided into separate soup and fish courses, and the carving to be done at the side-table, for the process to be complete.

Having said that, the main elements of *à la Française*, including the placing of dishes of various foods in the centre of the table, the habit of diners helping one another to the contents of these dishes, and the carving of the joint by the host at the head of the table, are continued in many households today, especially for the Sunday or Christmas dinners, which still retain some of the old traditions in a generation more accustomed to snacks and informality.

As polite society proceeded from dining *à la Française* to dining *à la Russe*, its etiquette, tableware, menus and mealtimes were rapidly adopted by the growing middle classes, especially the *nouveaux riches* who thrived in the mid-nineteenth-century expansion of industry, commerce and empire. In their homes the most fashionable and lavish lifestyle had to be demonstrated whenever company was present, even though this might impose penurious frugality when the family was not on show.

Further down the social scale, among the small farmers, craftsmen, agricultural workers and factory hands, things were greatly different. Since social, geographical and occupational mobility were still very restricted, they were relatively unaffected by fashion. Instead, they continued in routines which experience had proved to be the best for their particular ways of life and levels of income. This led to dinner being an extremely varied meal in mid-nineteenth-century England, as may be seen in the following examples.[21]

In the homes of north country coalminers, dinner had to be ready for serving directly the men arrived from the pit around 3.00 to 5.00 p.m. This meal, usually of roast meat, potatoes, fresh vegetables and Yorkshire pudding, was served to the whole family who sat around a number of tables in their living room/kitchen. The plates were of good-quality factory-made earthenware, and the knives, forks and spoons of fine Sheffield manufacture. Ceremony was cut to the minimum, as the vegetables were served directly from the pan on to the plate, although the meat was probably carved at the table.

In contrast, the farm servants who were boarded in the farmhouses of the East Riding of Yorkshire sat down to their dinner at a single long table in the farm kitchen. This was no ordinary table, however, for before each place a plate-sized hollow some two inches (5 cm) deep was carved out of its upper surface. It was customary for no cutlery to be laid on the table, each person carrying their own spoon and clasp-knife. At the start of the meal, the head of the household served the food from the head of the table following a strict order of precedence, first the head horseman (who counted as the second man on the farm, after the head of the household), then the third and fourth men on the farm, and then their respective lads. Broth or similar liquid foods were spooned into each hollow, but when roasts were served, the skilled carver would flick each slice from the point of his knife directly to each place in turn. Once these had been finished, the men helped themselves to a slice of fruit pie using a very precise technique. Holding the plate steady with two fingers of the left hand on the edge of the pie, the first cut was made from the centre to the left-hand side of the fingers, a second cut then being made from half an inch short of the centre to the right side of the fingers. As each succeeding cut was made anti-clockwise around the pie, a hexagonal piece was left in the centre, which thus ensured that everyone received the same proportion of crust to filling. At the end of the meal, the whole table was usually washed with hot water and soda, although in some households it was simply scoured with wisps of straw.

For the rural poor in upland Pennine communities, life at this period could be extremely hard. The nearest thing to a dining table was a small, rough, round three-legged affair accompanied by one or two old chairs; the total tableware was an old teapot and milk jug, two or three tea-cups, saucers and plates, and a few pint-sized, brown-glazed mugs called mess-pots, while for cutlery there were only one or two old kitchen knives, or perhaps none at all. Here the dinner served at midday was simply a pulp made of fried suet mashed with water, salt and boiled potatoes, all served in mess-pots, and eaten with oatcake, the occasional piece of fried bacon being considered a rare luxury.

At the very bottom of the social scale, the occupants of the overcrowded insanitary cellar-dwellings of the inner-city slums rarely dined in any sense of the word which we would recognize today. There was little opportunity for preparing even the most basic of meals, or of observing the simplest of social niceties in homes such as the following, observed in Bradford in 1849 by Angus Reach. It was 'a low, dark, foul-smelling place, with rough stools, and a broken table or so lying about; coarse crockery, either unwashed or full of dirty water, knives, without handles, and forks with broken prongs; bits of loaves smeared over by dirty hands; bundles of rags, buckets of slops, and unmade beds huddled on the stone or earthen floors in the corners'. Here the diet of bread, tea or coffee, and, very rarely, a little poor-quality meat, tended to be eaten at the convenience of the inhabitants, without the formality of regular mealtimes.

Superficially, these descriptions of working-class dinners might appear to be of little more than general antiquarian interest, but on more detailed inspection they are found to contain a number of revealing features. First, it will be seen that the term 'dinner' was still reserved for the main midday meal, even though it had left this hour by the opening of the eighteenth century in polite households, becoming firmly established in the early evening by the 1850s. Only recently in the course of the last ten years has dinner become largely accepted in England as a mid-evening meal, demonstrating the great time-lag between working-class and polite usage. In a completely different way, the table manners described in the rural East Yorkshire farmhouse demonstrate an even more remarkable time-lag, since they are those which were in polite use in the late medieval period, especially such features as the two-fingered left-hand grip on the food being cut, and the use of the knife, which are clearly described in sources such as the mid-fifteenth-century *Boke of Nurture* written by John Russell.[22]

In contrast, the descriptions of the industrialized urban dinners show that they were very much creations of their own time, owing little to earlier customs and practice. Where money was readily available, as in the miner's household, modern tableware and cutlery were used in a manner similar to the usage in middle-class homes; but where there was great poverty, virtually all the traditions of more prosperous times rapidly evaporated, degenerating to such an extent that bread was simply torn off the loaf, stuffed into the mouth, and swilled down with highly adulterated teas and coffees. Nothing could establish such a vivid contrast with the elaborate dinners described earlier in this chapter, or illustrate more clearly the social differences which characterized life in mid-Victorian England.

SIX

À LA RUSSE: THE NEW WAY OF DINING

VALERIE MARS

DINING LIKE RUSSIANS?

Dining *à la Russe*, a new, more structured way to dine, was to become fashionable as the nineteenth century progressed, eventually replacing the previous dining style, *à la Française*. This new arrangement in the way to serve dinner was integral to changes in the whole style of dinner-giving. *A la Russe*, as interpreted in Victorian dining circles, was a paradigm for both formal and informal rules which defined the diners in relation to one another and to the outside world. Those who gave *à la Russe* dinners had to employ more labour and acquire more glass and cutlery than had been necessary for dining *à la Française*.

How and why did the fashion in how dinners were served change so radically in the nineteenth century? Why should a Russian fashion have been taken up

112

when there were no other Russian influences on the way food was cooked or eaten?

A.L. Kirwan, the author of *Host and Guest*, comments in 1864 on how much more civilized the Russians became after Peter the Great – that was, after 1697:[1]

and even since 1815, but no sensible Englishman would think of going to Russia to learn to serve a dinner. . . . I spent much time in Russia somewhat more than thirty years ago and lived a great deal among Russians of wealth and position, but though there was wealth and profusion and a great deal of expenditure at their dinners, there was nothing like elegance or good taste. The earlier Russian cookery of a century ago was adopted from the Dutch and Germans and all that is valuable in the later Russian cookery has been adopted from the French and English kitchens.[2]

Kirwan was creating a false spectre, for dining *à la Russe* as practised in England took only its name and basic structure from the Russian original, and it was considerably adapted to fit English requirements. The extreme examples of dinner *à la Russe* and *demi-Russe*[3] that follow are from the Russian Ambassador's English maître d'hotel and two pocket etiquette books for new diners. These contrast with a menu of the early 1880s from one of the Sambournes' dinners. Linley Sambourne became chief cartoonist for *Punch*. Those with whom they reciprocated dinners were of the same social status, such as Luke Fildes RA, the 'genre' painter.

There was a set of rules to be followed from arrival to departure that could have only slight variations between different dining circles. The whole structure of *à la Russe* dining imposed a formal etiquette that overtly divided those who knew how to dine from the rest. Formal etiquette became important as it became more necessary to maintain social distance. This was reinforced by the meal's being served by servants rather than through the handing of food among the party. If a dish was refused, the refusal was not made directly to the dinner-giver; the impersonal service of servants mediated between hosts and guests. This represented the very opposite of the assumed intimacy of shared conviviality inherent in the structure of service *à l'Anglaise* or *à la Française*. None of the advice in later etiquette books directed at more experienced diners is to assist those 'not so much used to company', as Martha Bradley had written in 1760.[4] This was a more competitive milieu.

On entering the dining room, the diners would have seen at once that the dinner was to be served *à la Russe*. Arrangements of candelabra, flowers and dessert would be displayed down the middle of the table, taking the place of the dishes of food forming the courses and the removes of service *à la Française*. The table was also set with salt-cellars, water carafes and at each place, or between each two places, a menu. Menus were always written either in French or in a combination of French and English. A place setting would comprise a set of at least three wineglasses for the different wines served with each course, separate sets of cutlery and flatware for several courses, and a bread roll wrapped in a dinner napkin folded in one of the many fashionable styles.

As there were no dishes on the table, diners could no longer help themselves and each other, as in the previous style, but depended entirely on butlers, footmen, or parlourmaids to serve them. Carving was usually done by the butler from a sideboard or table. When the host carved the service was sometimes called '*demi-Russe*'. All wine was poured by servants, and only in some circles, after all the other dishes had been served, were the diners allowed to serve themselves dessert. After dessert, women left for the drawing room, as before, and men stayed behind to drink port before joining them later. The many subtle variations in how *à la Russe* was served insulated diners in their various social circles, and defined each as a relatively exclusive constituency. The description that follows is a basic outline to define how dinner *à la Russe* differed from *à la Française*, or *à l'Anglaise* as it was described more precisely by some chefs and commentators.

MULTIPLE COURSED DINNERS BEFORE *À LA RUSSE* WAS ESTABLISHED

Dining *à la Russe* was not a new invention. Prince Puckler Muskau, when writing home to Germany in 1826, remarked on the German fashion for dinners where dishes were passed by servants.[5] Thomas Cosnett in 1825 gives instructions not only for how a footman is to serve diners with plated meat, but also how he is to serve vegetables to each diner.[6] This does not seem to have been common practice, since Prince Puckler Muskau describes it as a German and not an English fashion. When writing about English dinners he describes the usual *à la Française* way of serving. Serving dishes in succession instead of simultaneously was not unknown to the French. François Marin, in

1739, in *Les Dons de Comus*, describes a supper with nine services of two or three dishes in each.[7] At the beginning of the next century, Grimod de la Reynier (1758–1809) gives an account of being visited by friends from Lyons, and of their eating four dishes in succession.[8] His Jury Degustateur, which met 465 times from 1803 to 1813, was always served dishes in succession.[9] These were submitted blind by restaurateurs and caterers to be commented on in the *Almanach des Gourmands*, thus establishing the idea of successive dishes, particularly for those who wished to taste food at its best.

À *LA RUSSE* ARRIVES IN ENGLAND

Charles Pierce, who was maître d'hotel at the Russian Embassy in London when he wrote his book, *The Household Manager*, in 1857, gives this description and origin for the name. 'Service à la Russe derived from the Czars' mode of dining' and 'was first introduced into France and England at the peace of 1814, out of compliment to the Emperor of Russia'.[10] This dinner was given by the Lord Mayor and Corporation of the City of London for the Prince Regent and the Emperor of Russia and the King of Prussia on 18 June 1814, but the records of the organizing committee do not indicate clearly that it was served *à la Russe*,[11] and two eminent artists who recorded the scene do not provide corroboration either. Luke Clennell's painting shows the dessert course, with the high table decorated by many silver-gilt pieces (there are indications that City merchants lent their domestic silver, too); and William Daniell depicted the diners in the main body of the hall eating *à la Française*, with the distant high table indiscernible.

The table decor had a propagandizing function, for it symbolized the power and wealth of the City of London. Table decor was an important part of dinners served *à la Russe*, which required display pieces to fill the spaces that in service *à la Française* would have been occupied by dishes of food from which diners helped themselves and their neighbours. However, when the same committee arranged a dinner for the Duke of Wellington some three weeks later, the service was in two courses, according to the records[12] (whereas two courses are not mentioned for the earlier dinner). Nothing is said of loaned silver either, but then the duke was not a foreign visitor to be impressed by City power.

The necessity to attribute the beginning of *à la Russe* to 1814 owes more to the Victorian love of classification than to the shedding of a true light on by whom, when and where dinners began to be served *à la Russe*. Abraham Hayward studied the dining tastes of wealthy and noble gastronomes and in his book, *The Art of Dining*, in 1852, describes an *à la Russe* dinner at Sir J.M. Stanley Errington's country house where he says it was 'most pleasingly and originally put into practice'. He comments, 'The service *à la Russe* divides the opinions of the best judges',[13] and so Hayward avoids becoming involved in the controversy that accompanied its introduction.

Another cautious advocate was Felix Urbain Dubois, French chef to the King of Prussia, some of whose books were translated from their original French editions, and who with Emile Bernard wrote *La Cuisine Classique*, 1856.[14] In their introduction they make out a case for service *à la Russe* on the grounds that it allowed the food to be served fresh and hot. They do, however, cater for their readers who prefer service *à la Française*, and advise the use of hot cupboards and hot-water dishes instead of *à la Russe*. Dubois in *Artistic Cookery* (1870) says, 'The adoption of service *à la Russe* is now-a-days a settled matter.'[15] Dubois was, however, largely addressing rich cosmopolitan diners, who formed only one group among the insulated range in styles of dinner-giving in England's new fragmented class-based society. It is not reasonable, therefore, to give an immovable date for the change to dining *à la Russe* in England.

Mrs Beeton in *The Book of Household Management* (1861) advised against dinners *à la Russe* in households without sufficient resources, suggesting that her readers for the most part were not among the most fashionable:

> Dinners *à la Russe* are scarcely suitable for small establishments; a large number of servants being required to carve and to help the guests; besides there being a necessity for more plates, dishes, knives, forks and spoons than are usually to be found in any other than a very large establishment. Where, however, a service à la Russe is practicable, there is perhaps no mode of serving a dinner so enjoyable as this.[16]

The pocket book *How to Dine* (1879) was written to supply a comparable readership's need, as was the chapter on 'The Dinner Party' in another pocket book, *Etiquette for Ladies*, published in 1894. Often 1890 is cited as the generally accepted date for *à la Russe* to have become the usual way to dine, but as Victorian social circles tended to be mutually exclusive, to make a generalization about the universal adoption of *à la Russe* is unhelpful. At the beginning of the 1880s the Sambournes and their circle were certainly giving *à la Russe* dinner parties.

THE RUSSIAN AMBASSADOR IN LONDON DINING
À LA RUSSE

The maître d'hotel, Charles Pierce, a friend of Alexis Soyer, was in 1857 writing for grander diners than Mrs Beeton's readers. She assumed in her chapter on 'Domestic Servants' that her readers did not employ any male servant above the status of butler, and she made no references to house stewards or maîtres d'hotel. The following quotations, however, are from Pierce's *Le Diner à la Russe* which gives all the characteristics of later Victorian dining.[17]

> A table, in size proportional for the number of guests invited is prepared, leaving scope for taste to display its decoration. The Russians prefer the round table. . . . Choicely-printed *menus* are placed by the plate of each guest. . . . Natural flowers, either cut or in roots, are placed in glass, in china, or in silver vases along the centre of the table.

Most English dinners are shown laid out on rectangular tables, as these were easier to expand with additional wooden 'leaves' for larger parties. Lesser dinner-givers than those enjoying ambassadorial hospitality could buy cards in assorted styles and write the menu themselves. Suggested floral arrangements ranged from simple vases of flowers to exotic arrangements of palms, ferns, mosses and festoons of flowers and smilax, with dessert placed among the arrangements.

The mode of laying the cloth is, that the lay-overs, or slips, are placed so as to extend no further than a few inches beyond the plate of each guest, and, at the same time, avoid all interference with the dessert.

This allowed easy removal of the slips when dessert was later served. It was no longer either fashionable or practical to serve dessert on bare mahogany.

Fine and rare fruits of various kinds are usually chosen for the dessert, for the pleasure they afford by their contrasting beauty.

The ornaments, be they with or without a plateau, are, as usual, placed in the centre of the table, and the dessert is placed symmetrically around them; taste, at times, prefers that the *hors-d'oeuvres* be not placed upon the table, but be offered from the side table; and in such cases less of them in quantity are required. . . .

The *hors-d'oeuvres* may be chosen from any of the following, or the like – as, fresh caviare, anchovies, pickled oysters, Dutch herrings, sardines, pickled tunny, prawns, lobsters, smoke-dried ham, and smoked salmon. . . . Thin slices of white and brown bread-and-butter, with dry toast and pats of butter, should also be in the room.

Small liqueur-glasses of Kumël de Riga, Cognac, Absinthe, and the like, are provocatives for the

dinner previously to the serving of soups. . . .
Beautiful specimens of small china, or of glass
dishes, can be brought into use to receive the *hors-
d'oeuvres*, and impart at the same time increase of
embellishment and ornament to the table.

Hors-d'oeuvres were a particularly Russian item that
was also served in England, oysters and lemon with
brown bread and butter being a favourite. Another
delicacy favoured in England was 'kippered salmon'
from Scotland. Drinking spirits with hors-d'oeuvres,
however, remained an exclusively Russian practice.
Where ingredients were simple, the growing emphasis
on, and need for, elaboration was supplied by the
tableware. *A la Russe* tables gave plenty of scope for
Victorian decorative wares.

At large dinners there were choices in all the courses.

THE FIRST COURSE

The company being seated, and the *hors-d'oeuvres*
having been handed, the soup being in the room,
the dinner commences being served from the side-
table; when the soup having been served, Sherry
and Madeira are generally offered with it.

Should turtle soup be present, the green-fat,
lemon, and cayenne should accompany it, and the
iced punch, as usual at the dinner *à l'Anglaise*.

With the earlier style, turtle soup was seen as an
indispensable component at festive English dinners. In
cosmopolitan circles dinner *à la Française* and *à
l'Anglaise* are described with only minor differences,
such as turtle soup.

Following the soups are the *petits pâtés*, or hot *hors-d'oeuvres* of any kind; after which the steward having portioned the fish for handing (which, if cod or turbot, is usually sliced), it is presented to each guest, having at the same time the sauces, potatoes, &c., handed by a servant following.

Sauterne, Graves, Chablis, or Sherry are the usual wines served with the fish.

The *relevés* of meat are served in the like way as the fish, these being also carved at the side-table, and presented in small dishes with gravy, which is followed by their appropriate vegetables. With the *relevés*, such wines as Chambertin, Bordeaux, or if more suitable, others, to the host's taste, are partaken of. The *entrées* next succeed. The finest Clarets are offered with them.

The term *relevé* described what had previously been called a remove, a large joint of meat or game. *Entrées* were sauced dishes of meat, game or poultry, of the type described in the earlier service as side dishes.

If the cold *hors-d'oeuvres* were placed upon the table at the commencement of the dinner, they should by this time be removed.

The roasts, such as game and choice poultry, which have been also carved at the side-table, are now served, accompanied by salad, together with the small pickled cucumber of Russia. . . .

Champagne, with either *punch à la Russe*, *à la Beaufort*, or *à la Brunnow*, should now be offered; yet, according to the taste of the company, other wines may be chosen, and so throughout the dinner.

Russian pickled cucumbers were unlikely to appear on English menus *à la Russe*. The punches were not drinks, but wine-based, lemon-flavoured ices or sorbets. They were taken to refresh the palate.

> The *entremets* are next offered, and should be served by the servants beginning with those of vegetables, and terminating with the sweet *entremets* of pastries, jellies, and the like.

These light dishes had previously all been served as one course. Under the new style sweet and savoury were now served separately as two distinct courses. Separation and classification were increasingly intrinsic to Victorian domestic organization, as they were becoming to all other aspects of living and working:

> with the vegetable *entremets*, the Hock or other Rhine wines are offered, – but the sweet *entremets* are accompanied by Champagne or other light wines. The hot *entremets* are first handed round, then the jellies, then the *entremets glacé*, such as *poudin à la Nesselrode*, &c. &c. &c.
>
> Where there have been no *soufflés*, the *fondue* is always served as the last dish, after which, cheese is or is not served, as may be wished; but if served, it is accompanied by Port wine, and occasionally by bottled porter or ale.
>
> The table is now cleared of the plates, glass, salts, lay-overs, &c., and succeeded by the dessert-plates and clean glasses; following which, –
>
> The dessert is drawn forward near to the guests, and presented, beginning with fresh fruits, and

followed by *compotes*, but reserving the sweets and *bon-bons* to be handed last.

A dessert course that was tightly structured could not be left for the diners to help themselves as previously. Dessert was now subsumed into the structure of dinner.

> The ices next are placed upon the table before the host, and served, the steward receiving the same from him, and passing them on by the servants to each guest, accompanied by ice-wafers and liqueur wines, as required by taste.
>
> With the ices, it is usual to offer at least two sorts of liqueur wines for choice. Most of the Russian nobles have the ices handed round, without placing them upon the table; and this is done before serving the dessert, which should likewise be handed to each guest.

When dinner *à la Russe* was served in English households, the distinctly Russian details were forgotten.

> The finger- and mouth-glasses, on a plate, are now placed upon the table before each guest . . . when after their use, the host and guests rise, and assemble in the drawing-room, where they partake of coffee and the usual liqueurs.

Pierce's dinner disregards the English custom of men staying to drink wine in the dining room and women meanwhile taking coffee in the drawing room. Pierce's *à la Russe* was, as has been shown, Russian only in small details. Not only was the division of roles between male and female sharply defined, but dining *à la Russe* was a way to structure a dinner tightly, with rules for the time of dining, the pace of the meal, rules for how to serve it, how to eat it and to whom to speak. This new way of dining begat a torrent of didactic works, for every aspect of the event. Etiquette and household books' instructions read as idealistic views of a new fashion for outsiders, often with status symbols dropped in among the directions.

TWO INSTRUCTIVE POCKET BOOKS

Etiquette for Ladies (1894), a small pocket book, with a chapter for young women who were new to dinner *à la Russe*, shows that the new dining could be set up as a trial of social acceptability. This description of a fashionable dinner party was written for aspirant diners.

An invitation to dinner must always be considered in the light of a compliment, and it is also an acknowledgement that you belong to the same class as your entertainers. Every country has some particular test of this kind, and in England the invitation to dinner is the hall-mark of social equality.[18]

However, in such an entrepreneurial age there must have been a great deal of accidental rule-breaking. But if rules of etiquette could be used 'in evidence' for exclusion from established dining circles, they could also allow the *arriviste*, if important enough, as Benvenuto Cellini had been in an earlier age, to be 'above the law'. 'Fin Bec' in the 1868 *Epicure's Year Book* writes: 'guide books will never make ladies or gentlemen. A manual of etiquette in the possession of a diner out is almost *a pièce de conviction.*'[19]

Etiquette for Ladies guides the new diner through the whole intricate procedure:

> At large dinner parties there are generally name cards placed in the plate; at small ones the host remains standing at the end of the table until the guests are seated, so that he may show them where to sit.[20]

As the century proceeded large parties became more fashionable as a demonstration of wealth and status. Mrs Sambourne was unable to have so many to dinner. Her table seated only eight, which was a more usual number for her circle.[21]

> When you take your seat at the table you will find your serviette folded in some fantastic form upon your plate with your dinner roll inside it. First take off your gloves, put your table napkin on your knees, and place your roll at the left-hand side of your plate. Two large knives and three large forks, and a silver knife and fork for fish, are laid for each person, together with a tablespoon for eating soup with. At your right-hand side is a group of glasses – a wide one for champagne, a small one for sherry, and a coloured one for hock.[22]

Separate silver or silver-plate fish knives and forks came into use after 1850; earlier, fish had been eaten with a silver fork and a piece of bread. Soup spoons were a later innovation, so that changing fashions among different dining circles could create further difficulties for outsiders. The choice of glasses caused no difficulties for the diner as the footman knew which glass to fill.

Your dessert-spoon and fork are not placed upon the table until the sweets appear. If salad is served you will have a separate plate (probably in the shape of a crescent); it will be placed at the left side of your plate. Use both plates at once, eating the salad off one and the meat off the other.

The first course to make its appearance now is usually some description of *hors-d'oeuvres*. Sometimes a few oysters are served, or else a china dish with three partitions is handed round, each partition containing a separate article, such as prawns, olives, or anchovies. You take which you prefer, and eat it on a little plate with a small knife and fork. After this comes soup, then fish, and next the *entrées*, then meat, fowl, game, and sweets. Help yourself slowly and calmly, and then you are not likely to spill anything upon the cloth. Some young ladies get into the foolish habit of passing a number of dishes because they are not quite sure how they should be helped. This is a very silly practice, for if they do so they will never learn.

The act of giving and receiving food was now limited to the servant and the diner, as compared to dining *à la Française* where diners had helped one another. Since almost all that could be handed by servants was now delegated to them, the result was an ostentatious (and silent) labour-intensity that considerably reduced interaction between the diners. Social distance buttressed by formal rules: this became integral to *à la Russe* dinners. Simple rules as to the order in which to use cutlery were now not enough; much more complicated rules relating the utensil to the food offered a further 'ordeal' in this social trial by dinner.

All *entrées*, such as patties, or mince, must be eaten with a fork only; but when sweetbreads, cutlets or game enter into the composition of the dish, a knife is of course requisite. Pastry is usually eaten with the fork alone, but a spoon must be used if fruit is in question.

A silver slice is an example of yet another specialized item that the new dinner-giver had to acquire in order to serve a fashionable dinner. Mrs Beeton referred to basic items, but for the most fashion-conscious there was an ever increasing number of types and styles of tableware to acquire.

When the sweets have been discussed the table is made ready for dessert. The crumbs are removed with a silver slice; the wineglasses are taken away, and three fresh ones (for claret, port and sherry) placed beside each person; the fruit, already on the table, is handed round by the servants, after a dessert-plate, containing a finger-glass on a d'oyley, together with a dessert-knife and fork, has been placed before each person. You must remove the finger-bowl from your plate, placing it on the d'oyley on the left side of your plate, a little to the front.

For nearly all kinds of fruit you require the assistance of the dessert-knife.

Drinking different wines was now integrated into the precisely structured courses. Fruit was classified by the way each category was eaten. To use cutlery when fingers are the rule immediately suggests the over-genteel rather than the ladylike; yet another trap for new diners.

Peaches are eaten with a spoon and fork. Pears, apples, and oranges are peeled and cut into halves and quarters, and eaten with the knife and fork. Pineapple and melon are treated in much the same manner. The skin of bananas should be stripped off downwards, and the fruit cut into small pieces. Raspberries, gooseberries, and currants are eaten with the fingers.

The same applies to strawberries, except they are taken with cream.

The strength of rules and formality continues, but contrasts with a luxurious studied carelessness showing that folding napkins for the next meal was not necessary.

When the ladies appear to have finished their dessert, the hostess gives the signal to retire. This she does by bowing to the lady on her husband's right hand, and rising from her seat. All the ladies then leave the room, the lady of highest rank going first, the unmarried ladies last, the hostess herself bringing up the rear.

Do not fold your table-napkin, but leave it on the chair you have vacated.

The ladies now repair to the drawing-room, when coffee is handed round to them almost at once. It is usually handed by two servants, the first bringing a tray with hot milk and sugar, the second the coffee. Tea is afterwards served on the arrival of the gentlemen, and is sometimes handed round, sometimes poured out by the hostess.

The men would already have had their coffee in the dining room and then joined the women in the drawing room, uniting the diners before the evening ended with a symbolic piece of hospitality.

The second description of a grand dinner in *demi-Russe* style, is from another tiny pocket book called *How to Dine*, published in 1879. Etiquette books were plentiful in a fast-changing time when outward manners were seen as a mirror of character. The following selections from instructions for a fashionable dinner party are written as if this rich and elaborate style of dining was to be generally admired. However, although it has all the sycophantic symptoms of status worship, ostentatious dining was also frequently a vehicle for criticizing the *nouveaux riches*.

A FASHIONABLE DINNER PARTY

At a fashionable dinner party the following were the arrangements. The guests were twenty-four in number . . . they began to assemble at half-past seven punctually. They were received in the library, where the host and hostess were standing ready to receive them, introducing those who were strangers to each other. When all had arrived the butler entered, and, going up to the lady of the house, told her, in a low voice, that dinner was served.[23]

Punctuality continued to be important, as it had been at the beginning of the century. More usually guests were received not in the library but in the drawing room; a status point is made by suggesting a room not possessed by most readers. But many practices in the new etiquette books were little different from accounts in earlier books. Much ideal instruction, particularly for servants, was unchanged; the new style of dining demanded technical changes rather than change in how servants conducted themselves.

Precedence was strictly observed. Ideally it would have been possible to pair up all the diners, but when there were odd single diners they were placed at the back of the procession. In the Sambournes' house, going down the narrow stair from the drawing-room in pairs would have been a tight fit.

> The hostess then arranged those that were not previously acquainted, and the gentlemen conducted the ladies to the dining-room, the principal stranger taking the mistress of the house, and the master giving his arm to the chief of the female guests.
>
> Going into the dining-room, the company passed by the butler and eight footmen, all of whom were stationed in two rows.[24]

For those who could not afford enough help, *The Ladies' Guide* of 1861 gives a method of using limited staff to maximum advantage to put on a dinner *à la Russe*:

> There might be a sort of drill exercise as follows: Whilst guests are being seated, a person outside brings up soup.

Footman receives soup at the door.

Butler serves it out.

Footman hands it.

Both change plates.

Footman takes out soup, and receives fish at door, whilst butler hands wines.

Butler serves out fish.

Footman hands it (plate in one hand, and sauce in the other).

Both change plates.

Footman brings in entrée, whilst butler hands wine.

Butler hands entrée.

Footman hands vegetables.

Both change plates.

And so on.

The carving of the joint seems the only little difficulty: this must be placed on the table and be carved by the host; should, however, this be thought too much of a return to a departing custom, the delay required to cut eight portions at the side-table would not prolong the dinner unreasonably: if the society is pleasant, where is the need of hurry?[25]

In all but the larger establishments, dinner parties could considerably increase the workload of the staff. Extra staff, particularly butlers and footmen, were therefore brought in. They were not always butlers and footmen by day – re-employed greengrocers were a favourite, and there were frequent jokes about greengrocers as waiters. Cre-fydd advises in her cookery book (1866): 'Respectable waiters and daily cooks are recommended by Bright Woodward Ironmongers, 182 Albion Place, Hyde Park Square.'[26]

At the grand *demi-Russe* dinner described below carving is given a formality in keeping with the rest of the evening. Carving demonstrated a potent and symbolic act, with inferences of power and incorporation.

> Afterwards a saddle or haunch of Welsh mutton was placed at the **master's end** of the table, and at the **lady's end** a boiled turkey.
>
> These dishes being removed to the side-tables, very thin slices of each were handed round.[27]

Red meat at his end and white meat at hers symbolized male and female distinctions. Not to put joints on the table was a dilemma for *à la Russe* dinner-givers since it removed this highly charged and symbolic icon from the central viewpoint of the diners. In 1890 Dr Walsh says of dinner *à la Russe*: 'The latter is, however, greatly modified, and altered on the Russian model, but still it does not throw the duties of carving on the servant.'[28]

> Ham and tongue were then supplied to those who took poultry; and currant jelly to eaters of mutton. Next came the vegetables, handed round on dishes divided into four compartments, each division containing a different sort of vegetable.
>
> Next, two dishes of game were put on – one before the master of the house, and the other before the mistress. The game (which was perfectly well done) was helped by them and sent round with appropriate sauce to be eaten with the salad. After this, port wine – the Champagne being early

in the dinner. Next, the sweets were handed round. With the sweets were frozen fruits – fruits cut up and frozen with **isinglass jelly** (red, in moulds). On a side-table were Stilton and cream cheese.[29]

This course was served as had been fashionable at earlier *à la Française* dinners. Sweet and savoury were not as sharply divided as in true *à la Russe*. Male and female distinctions are also symbolized in the choice of cheese on offer: masculine equates with age, colour and strong flavour, and feminine with the new, white and mild. The servants do not leave the diners during dessert as they had done previously in the informality of *à la Française*. Now a limited informality was a privilege reserved for the men who were attended only by the most important servant, but spent 'not more than a quarter of an hour over the fruit and wine'.[30]

Time governed the evening. How different from the earlier style where time was not emphasized. Informal good-fellowship would not have had much opportunity to flourish in a circumspect fifteen minutes.

THE FOOD

How was the menu filled? To produce a dinner that had to be so different from an everyday dinner meant quite a lot of food and services being brought in for the occasion. But the new way of dining also meant a change in the way food was chosen, cooked and served. If the food was served by servants, the structure of timing demanded by successive courses meant that dishes had to be easily portioned out. If they were handed round on a dish and diners were to help themselves, then it must be made immediately apparent to them what constituted a portion.

Marion Sambourne, the wife of Linley Sambourne, the *Punch* cartoonist, kept a notebook of dinner menus served at home and at some of the dinners they attended. Her complimentary comments and descriptions are mostly of labour-intensive and decorative dishes she ate as a guest. Their everyday dinners, although cooked by a cook, were plain. The contrast is marked: an ordinary dinner, 12 July 1882, comprised 'sardines, curried mutton, cold beef, tomato salad, blancmange'. Compare this with the dinner for eight they served to guests on 2 May: 'oysters, brown bread and butter, clear soup, salmon, sharp sauce, cucumber, lobster cutlets, chaufroid of pigeon, fricandeau of lamb, cauliflowers, new potatoes, asparagus, quails, salad, baba of rhum, compote of fruit, cream, New Forest cheese, anchovies, etc.'.[31] As *à la Russe* dining changed from fashionable exclusivity to become the accepted norm, dinner was adapted to the tastes and status of each dining circle. The Sambournes and their circle usually had menus of the same number of courses, often with common items such as consommé or clear soup. Consommé was a popular item as it was easy to make according to a range of standards.

At the grandest dinners the new way of dining was well served by the prevailing French cuisine, and the food was frequently cooked by French chefs. Dinner *à la Russe* had a set menu which required a particular repertoire of dishes in a suitably elaborate form that was easy to portion. Towards the end of the century, Mrs Marshall and Mrs de Salis produced pseudo-French culinary elaboration that was designed for lesser level *à la Russe* menus. Mrs Marshall ran a cookery school where her short courses included a day devoted to producing a dinner *à la Russe*.[32] If her pupils or their employers hadn't the resources to cook a whole dinner, the enterprising Mrs Marshall sold menu fillers like jars of consommé and pickled herrings, for *hors-d'oeuvres*, as well as food colours and gelatine for making food look decorative.

At the end of the century, Mrs de Salis wrote a series of cookbooks – all with '*à la mode*' in the title. The dishes were in an eclectic, elaborate style but were not too difficult to assemble. Her elaboration has more in common with the repertoire of 'pseudo-French' menus than true French cuisine.

This move to elaboration and the disguising of food in its natural form was part of a flight to gentility. The woman who did not go to the kitchen but had to put on dinners in a new fashion demanded a cuisine that often had no place in her own culinary past, or that of the cook she employed. In one of the many tirades against this new cuisine, the anonymous author of *Dinners and Dinner Parties, or the Absurdities of Artificial Life* says it is unwise to dine where 'the lady of the mansion' has nothing to do with the cuisine,[33] for Victorian hostesses often relegated all the work of dinner-giving to servants or hired help, with the exception of ordering the dinner, possibly arranging the flowers and buying some of the more expensive dessert items.

'French-like' cuisine was an important part of *recherché* dinners. *Recherché* was a favourite term to describe French-based cuisine, whether the real thing or an imitation. In Charles Herman Senn's *Dictionary of Foods*, *recherché* is defined as 'exquisite – dainty'.[34] A meal that was exquisite and dainty was entirely in keeping with the refinements aspired to by lady dinner-givers. For these dinners only the choice of wine lay under the host's control, though grander books – such as Urbain Dubois' *Cosmopolitan Cookery*[35] – emphasized male gourmet choice for men who ordered dinner from their maître d'hotel or chef.

Dinner *à la Russe* gave plenty of scope for eclectic elaboration in both food and decor. The table decorations and the china and glass needed for giving a dinner were, it seems, often feminine choices. French plates with roses contrasted with plain white tableware which some male critics preferred.

Dining *à la Russe* turned the table into a mass of visual and ranked messages. Floral decorations should be 'choice' – a word used to suggest more expensive and rare goods. The silver could be solid or plate. After 1851 electroplate superseded Sheffield plate, and cutlery and flatware could be either monogrammed or crested – there was no bar in England to taking a crest. China and glass, too, came in several qualities and in an extremely wide range of designs.

What was particular about Victorian decorative choices was that they were not always chosen to be consistent with a single cultural ideal such as classicism, as had been the case in the eighteenth century, and as the choices would later become with the Art and Crafts movement. But contemporary with more artistic taste there also came a choice of kitsch artifacts in an eclectic mixture of styles. At the beginning of the century, silverware could be obtained in Egyptian, Grecian, 'Hindu', Rococo revival, Antiquarian and Gothic styles. Later in the nineteenth century, the range of dinner wares increased considerably and produced haphazard selections of different period styles. Crazes for motifs like cabbage roses, and those based on enthusiasms like fern collecting, were popular. Soyer suggested scenic dessert plates as they made good topics for conversation.[36] Diners could talk about their travels, and dessert plates would encourage competitive claims to having visited exotic places. Novelties for the table were also useful conversation pieces and could be an expression of the host's special interests. What was or was not appropriate to dinner-givers, was there to be 'read' by their guests and servants.

The table has always been there to be read, and the Victorians, like their forebears, could use heraldic devices to put over their messages. Further elaboration was increasingly accessible with the additional range of objects from world trade and industrial expansion. And if the dinner-giver did not own the right things, or enough of them, Searcy or any of the other caterers could give a choice of china, glass and silver plate for hire.

A la Russe dining, whether slightly modified into *demi-Russe* or at its most intricate, was ideally suited to the new Victorian class-ridden society. The use of space, time, objects, cuisine and labour governed by a complex etiquette defined those who dined in their appropriate social circles as opposed to those who did not. Any association with Russian customs was, by the end of the century, quite forgotten.

SEVEN

SUPPER: THE ULTIMATE MEAL

C. ANNE WILSON

Supper, the final meal event of the day, varied enormously in both timing and content in the Victorian period. For those who ate dinner at the end of the morning, supper took place in the early evening, a substantial meal where families were comfortably off, though less so than dinner. But for many people this pattern changed as high tea took on the role of a full-scale early evening meal at the end of the working day. The supper that followed high tea was both lighter and later, taken in mid-evening or shortly before bedtime.

For those who dined in the evening, supper could disappear altogether, to be replaced by the drinking of tea, served two or three hours after dinner, with cakes and sandwiches as an accompaniment for those requiring more solid fare. But if the evening diners were caught up in the social events of the season, and they went on after dinner to a reception, an 'at home', a soirée, a ball or other social entertainment, then the refreshment offered to guests during the latter part of the evening was an elegantly laid-out supper made up of a variety of cold dishes.

Supper took its name from the Old French *soupée*, the term for the equivalent last meal of the day in France. In Britain in medieval times it was consumed at what seems to us a remarkably early hour. The household ordinances of the Duke of Clarence drawn up in 1469 show that he and his household dined at ten o'clock in the morning in summer, and had supper at 5.00 p.m.; in winter dinner was moved back to nine o'clock and supper to 4.00 p.m.[1]

Very few supper menus survive from that period. From those that do, we can deduce that the suppers of the aristocracy and higher gentry comprised dishes similar to those eaten at dinner – meat or fish in many varieties, cooked in pottages, roasted or baked, and rich made dishes, tarts and custards.[2] Further down the social scale was the supper on offer to pilgrims at the inn at Canterbury:

> And ye shall have made, at your devis,
> A great pudding, or a round haggis,
> A French moile, a tansie or a fraise.[3]

(The moile was a confection based on animal marrow and grated bread, with seasonings; the tansie and the fraise were prepared from eggs strained and cooked with herbs.)

Those who could afford to eat meat twice a day continued in Tudor times to enjoy a supper which closely resembled dinner in its composition. Andrew Boorde, the Elizabethan physician, commented: 'Also

Englishmen feed on gross meates at the beginning of dinner and supper [i.e. in the first course], and when the good meate doth come to the table [i.e. the poultry, smaller birds, young rabbits, etc., of the second course] through feeding upon gross meate the appetite is extinct.' But since the sight of the second-course fare proved an irresistible temptation, men usually went on to eat the 'latter meate' in addition, 'whereupon doth come replecyon and surfets'.[4]

The earliness of the medieval and Tudor suppertime was a response to the need to make maximum use of the hours of daylight at a period when there was no gas or electricity to supply artificial light. But it left a gap before bedtime which encouraged people inclined to stay up late to insert a second supper, known as a rere-supper (from Old French *arrière soupée*). First recorded in 1303, this much later evening supper was a lighter meal. Eventually it came to be seen as almost equivalent to the Tudor and Stuart 'banquet' or dessert course of sugar-preserved fruits and other sweetmeats which was more usually served at the end of a festive dinner. Not surprisingly rere-suppers acquired the reputation of encouraging drunkenness and bad behaviour. But one reason why they died out early in the seventeenth century was that the other mealtimes had begun to move forward. A later dinner at noon or 1.00 p.m. led to a late supper, and people then found that their customary bedtime arrived before they were ready for a further meal, other than a nightcap of bread and ale.

The mealtime hours continued to advance through the next two centuries. Parson Woodforde, as his diary shows, dined regularly at 3.00 p.m. in the 1780s, with a hearty mid-evening supper to follow including hot cooked fowls, mutton or other meat foods. He found it remarkable when his niece visited friends on 22 October 1790 and 'they did not dine until near 6 o'clock in the evening', and when his own busy day on 6 November 1791 meant that 'it was near five o'clock this Afternoon before I could get to dinner'.

Yet in the early decades of the nineteenth century the five o'clock dinner hour became customary for the middle and gentry classes. The drinking of tea two or three hours after dinner had also become a very widespread practice, and this did not now take place until 7.00 p.m. or later. Since the tea, and sometimes coffee, was generally accompanied by cakes and sandwiches or bread and butter, further sustenance hardly seemed necessary until perhaps 10.00 p.m., and at that hour most people did not wish to embark on a substantial supper of hot cooked meat, fish, pies, puddings and other such food.

Mrs Rundell stated in her *New System of Domestic Cookery*, first published in 1806, 'Hot suppers are not much in use where people dine very late',[5] a view that was repeated in cookery books all through the nineteenth century. By the 1860s dinner had moved on further to 6.00 p.m. at least, and for some people to 6.30 p.m. or even 7.00 p.m., and Mrs Beeton wrote in 1861: 'Hot suppers are now very little in request, as people now generally dine at an hour which precludes the possibility of requiring supper, at all events not one of a substantial kind.' But should such a meal be needed, she suggested that a bill of fare for dinner 'with slight alterations will answer for a hot supper'.[6] Twenty years later, *Cassell's Dictionary of Cookery* did not offer even this concession, claiming that 'the modern practice of dining late has all but put an end to the hot, heavy suppers which were once so much in vogue. Nowadays supper partakes more of the nature of a light refreshment than of a solid meal.'[7]

The lighter meal accorded well with the advice of nineteenth-century physicians. Dr William Kitchiner in 1822 had advocated a small supper, following a five o'clock dinner and a drink of tea (but no solid food) two hours later. The final meal was to be 'a biscuit or a sandwich or a bit of cold fish, &c. and a glass of beer or wine and toast and water . . . as light a supper as possible'.[8] Similar advice was given in the separate medical section on supper-eating published in *The Dictionary of Daily Wants* in 1858, but total abstinence was not recommended: 'thus many a dyspeptic subject will find his morning meal better digested after a light supper than without one.'[9]

For the families who followed the fashionable evening dinnertime as it gradually slipped forwards, what happened was first of all that supper was replaced by a snack at bedtime ('a glass of negus, a biscuit or a sandwich' was suggested by Alexis Soyer in the 1840s).[10] Then, as dinnertime advanced further still, the regular tea-drinking that took place some two hours afterwards, with accompanying cakes or bread and butter, itself turned into the pre-bedtime snack. This was the pattern for the quiet family evening at home.

SUPPERS FOR ENTERTAINMENTS

But later hours were kept and a more substantial supper was served when an evening entertainment took place. Mrs Rundell had already set the scene for this meal in the early years of the nineteenth century. After setting out a long list of appropriate foods ('The top and bottom [of the table] may be either game, fowls, rabbit, boiled fish such as soles, mackerel, oysters stewed or scalloped', while elsewhere were laid 'French beans, cauliflower or Jerusalem artichokes, grated hung beef with butter, with or without rusks . . . custards in glasses with sippets, potted meat' and a great many more items), she made some suggestions for the overall appearance of the supper table and how to achieve it.

The brighter the things the better they appear, and glass intermixed has the best effect. Jellies, different coloured things and flowers add to the beauty of the table. An elegant supper may be served at small expense by those who know how to make trifles that are in the house form the greatest part of the meal.[11]

The cold supper, prepared ahead for a large number of guests, became an ideal area for the Victorians to indulge in their love of ornament and decoration. Mrs Beeton in 1861 pointed out that 'the odours and flavours of the various dishes should contrast nicely; there should be plenty of fruit and flowers on the table, and the room should be well lighted'. She recommended heavy use of garnishes: 'Hams and tongues should be ornamented with cut vegetable flowers, raised pies with aspic jelly cut in dice, and all the dishes garnished sufficiently to be in good taste without looking absurd.'[12] The eye, in fact, should be as fully gratified as the palate.

As the century moved on, so it became fashionable not merely to garnish food but also to give it a shiny, glossy appearance. *Cassell's Dictionary of Cookery*, about 1881, advised, 'Articles that will allow of it should be glazed and ornamented with artificial flowers, &c. Melted lard, thinned with a little salad oil, may be used for decorating hams and tongues. . . . Bright parsley, scraped horse-radish, cut lemon, red beetroots, hard-boiled egg, &c. will all be required for garniture.'[13] Six years later Major L. . . advocated either arranging cold fish, poultry, and game in aspic, or coating them with chaudfroix, a sauce made from good stock and cream mixed with an equal quantity of aspic jelly, which set to produce a glossy surface on the food.[14]

Hot soup was often served to start off a cold supper. Esther Copley in 1830 had described it as 'an addition to modern suppers which is often found particularly grateful and restoring'.[15] Mrs Beeton explained the method of service: 'Soup . . . is not placed on the table. The servants fill the plates from a tureen on the buffet, and then hand them to the guests: when these plates are removed, the business of supper commences.'[16]

Such suppers required a large table in a spacious room to accommodate many guests. A later alternative was to substitute a number of small tables. Major L. . ., offering menu suggestions for ball suppers in 1887, wrote: 'I should also strongly advise that suppers should be served on several small tables in preference to one large one, and that a dish of each sort should adorn each table.'

He was writing for the well-to-do in their large houses. But there were readers of a new type for cookery and household books during the Victorian era. The middle- and upper-class audience addressed by most of the cookery-book writers was constantly expanding as families prospered and aspired to rise in society. They learned from the books how to entertain on an ample scale, but they often did not live in homes that could easily accommodate great numbers of guests seated around tables. By the middle decades of Queen Victoria's reign Mrs Beeton was giving advice for the occasions 'when small rooms and large parties necessitate having a standing supper'. The standing or buffet supper (with much of the fare laid out on the buffet or sideboard) was an innovation that allowed the maximum number of people to be entertained in the minimum of space. The food had to be of a type suitable for consumption by the standing eater. Mrs Beeton's list of dishes for an entertainment of this sort was:

> Beef, ham and tongue sandwiches, lobster and oyster patties, sausage rolls, meat rolls, lobster salad, dishes of fowls, the latter *all cut up*; dishes of sliced ham, sliced tongue, sliced beef and galantines of veal; various jellies, blancmanges and creams; custards in glasses; compotes of fruit; tartlets of jam, and several dishes of small fancy pastry; dishes of fresh fruit, bonbons, sweetmeats, two or three sponge cakes, a few plates of biscuits, and the buffet ornamented with vases of fresh or artificial flowers.[17]

Patties filled with cooked cold meat or fish 'very nicely minced, suitably seasoned' were a favourite supper dish. 'If you can get from the pastry-cook empty puff patties, it will save you trouble', advised Anne Cobbett.[18]

In the larger towns it was possible also to purchase oysters, ready-cooked meat and fish, pies, cakes and many other items to help reduce the amount of kitchen work required to set up a supper. Bachelor suppers were often based entirely upon such convenient fare. Mr Bob Sawyer's supper in *Pickwick Papers* was designed to be such a meal, though unfortunately he forgot to have his oysters opened up by the purveyor and lacked a knife suitable to carve the beef and ham from the German sausage-shop around the corner, and so was obliged to feed his card-playing friends on strong cheese and porter. But Dickens here, as elsewhere, shows us how easy it was to obtain ready-to-eat foods in Victorian London.[19]

WORKING PEOPLE'S SUPPERS

At every level of society, supper in Victorian times was an evening meal. Working-class families continued to call the meal eaten in the middle of the day dinner, even when it comprised no more than bread with a little cheese or bacon for the father, and tea and bread for the mother and children. Supper would then be the most substantial meal, shared at home in the evening when the father and any older children who were employed elsewhere had returned.

A hot supper forming the main meal of a typical working family might consist of a little meat or fried bacon accompanied by potatoes or cabbage, carrots or turnips grown in the family's own small garden. For the better-off there was bread and butter or a plain pudding in addition. But where the workplace was close to home, allowing the family to have their dinner as their main meal at the end of the morning, that was the substantial hot meal, and supper was smaller, comprising bread and cheese, or bread and butter, or potatoes. Bread and cheese was the supper generally supplied to domestic servants (who always ate a main meal dinner at the end of their morning's work), with the alternative occasionally of bread and cold meat left over from hot joints served earlier to their employers.

But there were many who could not look forward to a substantial meal either at dinnertime or suppertime during the earlier years of Queen Victoria's reign. Agricultural labourers and their families suffered very badly in the 'hungry forties' and for many years afterwards, especially in the southern counties of England. For the worst off, supper, even when it was the main meal of the day, comprised either potatoes or bread, sometimes flavoured with a little dripping or bacon fat, and washed down by tea without milk.[20] In much of northern England and Scotland oatmeal and potatoes were the basic foods; the oatmeal was consumed as crowdie, hasty pudding and other forms of porridge and gruel, and it was also turned into oatcakes. Milk was, however, more readily available in northern Britain to add extra nourishment to the oatmeal dishes. Porridge with milk appears often as a supper on the diet sheets of Victorian workhouses in Yorkshire.[21]

The standard of living did eventually improve, at least for a large proportion of working-class families. Eating patterns changed, too, in a way which affected both the timing and content of supper. High tea, first adopted as a full-scale early evening meal in Scotland and northern England, was spreading to midland and southern provincial England and to Wales in the middle years of the nineteenth century. It became a meal not only for working-class families but also for those of the provincial middle classes, for it was a true family meal (unlike the more gentrified evening dinner from which children were often excluded). Inevitably high tea caused supper to become a smaller, later affair, more in the nature of a snack for the adults before their bedtime. Thus the editions of Mrs Beeton's *Book of Household Management* current during the 1880s recommended following a solid high tea at six or seven o'clock with a supper 'of a very light character, such as a glass of wine and a slice of cake, or the more homely glass of beer and bread and cheese'.[22]

Clearly supper was a very variable meal, in both timing and content, during Queen Victoria's reign. It could be light or heavy, a main meal or a late evening snack, a decorative showpiece for the society hostess or rough victuals set on a cottage table. The only common factor for Victorian suppers was that they formed the final episode of the day's eating.

NOTES

Introduction

1. J. Burnett, *Plenty and Want* (1966), p. 96. This book is very informative on many aspects of Victorian diet, both for the rich and the poor.
2. Ibid., pp. 203–13.
3. Ibid, pp. 100–3.

Chapter One

1. *A Collection of Ordinances and Regulations for the Government of the Royal Household . . .* (1790), *passim*.
2. Thomas Percy, *The Regulation and Establishment of the Household of Henry Algernon Percy, the Fifth Earl of Northumberland* (1905), pp. 73–7.
3. Andrew Boorde, *A Compendyous Regyment, or A Dyetary of Helth, 1542* (Early English Text Society, ES 10, 1870), pp. 251, 265.
4. William Harrison, *Description of England*, ed. F.J. Furnivall, *Part I* (1877), pp. 141–2, 162.
5. Nicholas Breton, *Fantasticks*, 'The 12 Houres' (1626), in his *Works*, ed. A.B. Grosart (1879), Vol. 2, section t, pp. 12–15.
6. *The Court and Kitchin of Elizabeth commonly called Joan Cromwel* (1664), pp. 56, 114–15.
7. Sir Kenelm Digby, *The Closet . . . Opened*, 3rd edn (1677), pp. 121, 134.
8. Robert Scott-Moncrieff, ed., *The Household Book of Lady Grisell Baillie, 1692–1733* (1911), p. xlvii.

9. J.H. Adeane, ed., *The Girlhood of Maria Josepha Holroyd* (1896), pp. 13–14.
10. Norman Scarfe, tr. and ed., *A Frenchman's Year in Suffolk, 1784* (Suffolk Records Society, Vol. 30, 1988), pp. 21–2.
11. Anne Cobbett, *The English Housekeeper*, 2nd edn (*c.* 1840), pp. 11, 12.
12. Anne Battam, *The Lady's Assistant in the Oeconomy of the Table*, 2nd edn (1759), pp. 287–8.
13. Charlotte Mason, *The Lady's Assistant for Regulating and Supplying her Table*, 2nd edn (1775), pp. 88–97.
14. Isabella Beeton, *The Book of Household Management* (1861), pp. 959 ('Breakfasts') and 824 ('Boiled Eggs').
15. Beeton, new edn (1869), p. iv.
16. Beeton, new edn (1880), pp. iv, 1232, 1233–5, 1243–4.
17. Beeton, new edn (1888), pp. 1308, 1317–24.
18. *The Breakfast Book* (1865), pp. v, 66.
19. Major L. . ., *Breakfasts, Luncheons and Ball Suppers* (1887), p. 22. He has been identified as Major James Henry Landon (1832–1915), an Inspector of the Board of Agriculture from 1886 to 1901.
20. *The Breakfast Book*, p. vi.
21. Major L. . ., pp. 1–2.
22. Ibid., p. 16.
23. Ibid., pp. 17–21.
24. Beeton (1880), pp. 1234 and 1243–4.
25. Major L. . ., p. 1.
26. Ibid., p. 2.
27. Beeton (1888), p. 1317.
28. M.L. Allen, *Breakfast Dishes for Every Morning of Three Months*, 14th edn (1892), p. v.
29. B. Seebohm Rowntree, *Poverty: A Study of Town Life*, new edn (1906), p. 266.
30. Ibid., p. 276.
31. Ibid., p. 289.
32. Ibid., p. 290.
33. Ibid., p. 291.
34. Gabriel Tschumi, as told to Joan Powe, *Royal Chef* (1954), pp. 47–8.
35. Ibid., p. 48.

36. *The Breakfast Book*, p. 13.
37. Ibid., p. 100.
38. Henry Southgate, *Things a Lady Would Like to Know*, 6th edn (1881), p. 425.
39. Beeton (1861), p. 959.
40. Beeton (1880), p. 1234.
41. Beeton (1888), p. 1318.
42. See J.M. Scott, *The Tea Story* (1964), for a history of tea.
43. Samuel Pepys, *Diary*, ed. R. Latham and W. Matthews, *Volume I – 1660* (1970), p. 253, entry for 25 September 1660.
44. G.G. Sigmond, *Tea: Its Effects, Medicinal and Moral* (1839), pp. 53–61.
45. Southgate, p. 427.
46. Sigmond, p. 82.
47. Cobbett, p. 13.
48. A. Kenney Herbert, *Fifty Breakfasts* (1894), p. 7.

Chapter Two

1. W. Kitchiner, *The Art of Invigorating and Prolonging Life*, 3rd edn (1822), pp. 20–1.
2. H.M. Pollard, 'A liquid diet', in *Liquid Nourishment*, ed. C.A. Wilson (1993), pp. 52–4.
3. L.F. Salzman, *Building in England* (1967), p. 79; R.E.G. Kirk, ed., *Accounts of the Obedientiars of Abingdon Abbey* (Camden Society publications, 51, 1892), p. 28.
4. *Burgh records, Stirling* (1887), Vol. I, p. 35, quoted in *Oxford English Dictionary*.
5. Quoted in J. Wright, *The English Dialect Dictionary* (1898), Vol. 1.
6. W. Ellis, *The Country Housewife's Family Companion* (1750), p. 76.
7. Wright, Vol. 1: 'bever'.
8. Ibid.
9. H. Mayhew, *London Labour and the London Poor* (1861), Vol. 3, p. 139.
10. *OED*: 'lunch'.
11. *OED*: 'luncheon'.

12. E. Ward, *Writings: a Collection of Historical and State Poems*, 3rd edn (1706), Vol. 2, p. 125.
13. M.E. Rundell, *A New System of Domestic Cookery*, new edn (1809), p. xiv.
14. J. Austen, *Letters*, ed. R.W. Chapman, 2nd edn (1952), pp. 195, 228.
15. J. Austen, *Pride and Prejudice*, ed. E.W. Bradbrook (1970), Vol. 2, Ch. 16, p. 197.
16. M. Edgeworth, *The Absentee* (1812), Part 2, pp. 34–5.
17. *OED*: 'luncheon'.
18. S. and S. Adams, *The Complete Servant* (1825), p. 237.
19. Ibid., p. 340.
20. T. Webster, *An Encyclopaedia of Domestic Economy* (1844), p. 333.
21. Ibid.
22. E.C. Gaskell, *North and South*, ed. D.W. Collin (Penguin edn, 1970), pp. 55–6.
23. A. Bowman, *The New Cookery Book*, 2nd edn (1869), p. 589.
24. Major L. . ., pp. 26, 39 ff.
25. A. Hope, 'Glamis Castle, Angus', in *Traditional Country House Cooking*, ed. C.A. Wilson (1993), p. 63.
26. Lord Macaulay, *Life and Letters*, ed. G.O. Trevelyan, quoted in A. Palmer, *Movable Feasts* (1952), p. 59.
27. *Cassell's Domestic Dictionary* (*c.* 1884), p. 733.
28. Ibid., p. 733.
29. Beeton (1861), p. 759.
30. A. Soyer, *The Modern Housewife*, 2nd edn (1849), p. 28.
31. Hope, p. 63.
32. Soyer, p. 29.
33. Beeton (1861), p. 859.
34. Ibid., p. 959.
35. *Cassell's Dictionary of Cookery* (*c.* 1881), p. 392.
36. K. Mellish, *Cookery and Domestic Management* (*c.* 1901), Vol. 2, p. 972.

NOTES

Chapter Three

1. Much of the background work on this area is documented in D. Attar, *Household Books Published in Britain, 1800–1914* (Prospect Books, 1987) and E. Driver, *Cookery Books Published in Britain, 1875–1914* (Prospect Books, 1989). I would like to pass heartfelt thanks on to these two researchers, and would also like to thank the librarians responsible for the Special Collections at the Brotherton Library, University of Leeds, for their help over the last two years.
2. Attar, p. 188.
3. Driver, pp. 540–70.
4. H. Fraser, *The Coming of the Mass Market, 1850–1914* (1981).
5. G. Boyce, and others, *Newspaper History* (1978).
6. Attar, p. 171.
7. For an account of the background to the mid-Victorian readership, see M. Beetham and others, *Women's Worlds: Ideology, Femininity and the Woman's Magazine* (1991).
8. Much of the technological history is clearly documented in C. White's classic, *Women's Magazines 1693–1968* (1970).
9. T. Richards, *The Commodity Culture of Victorian England: Advertising and Spectacle, 1851–1914* (1991).
10. For some relevant background, see L. Hunter, 'Nineteenth- and Twentieth-century Trends in Food Preserving: Frugality, Nutrition or Luxury', in *Waste Not, Want Not*, ed. C.A. Wilson (1991).
11. R. Altick, *The English Common Reader: a Social History of the Mass Reading Public, 1800–1900* (1957).
12. N. Armstrong, 'The Rise of the Domestic Woman', in *The Ideology of Conduct*, ed. N. Armstrong and L. Tennenhouse (1987).
13. For a background on the nineteenth-century family, see P. Laslett and R. Wall, *Household and Family in Past Time* (1972), C. Harris, *The Family and Industrial Society* (1983), and L. Davidoff and C. Hall, *Family Fortunes: Men and Women of the English Middle Class* (1987).
14. D. Vincent, *Literacy and Popular Culture in England, 1750–1914* (1989).

15. For background to the domestic life of women during this period, see J. Lewis, ed., *Labour and Love: Women's Experience of Home and Family, 1850–1940* (1986), S. Delamont and L. Duffin, eds, *The Nineteenth-century Woman: Her Culture and Physical World* (1978), and E. Whitelegg and others, eds, *The Changing Experience of Women* (1982).
16. Quoted from A. Oakley, *Housewife* (1976) by Attar, p. 12.

Chapter Four

1. W.H. Ukers, *All About Tea* (1935), Vol. 2, p. 405.
2. Beeton, new edn (1880), p. 1242.
3. W. Cobbett, *Cottage Economy*, stereotype edn (1822), pp. 13–15.
4. J.B. Priestley, *When We are Married: a Yorkshire Farcical Comedy* (1938), p. 8.
5. T. Short, *Discourses upon Tea* (1750; reprinted 1974), p. 46.
6. E.C. Gaskell, *Cranford* (1853; new edn 1980), p. 66.
7. C. Brontë, *Shirley* (1849; new edn, 1981), p. 114.
8. C. Dickens, *Barnaby Rudge* (1841; Mandarin edn, 1991), p. 718.
9. Priestley, p. 8.
10. See, for instance, J. Woodforde, *Diary of a Country Parson, 1758–1802*, ed. J. Beresford, 5 vols (1924–31).
11. M. Dods, *The Cook and Housewife's Manual*, 4th edn (1829), pp. 74–5.
12. Gaskell, *Cranford* (1980), p. 162.
13. *Mrs Beeton's Cookery Book*, new edn (*c.* 1910), p. 367. This book is a much altered later edition of *The Englishwoman's Cookery Book*, a compilation using material from *The Book of Household Management* and first published by Samuel Beeton in 1863. The cover title was *Shilling Cookery Book*. It was re-titled *Mrs Beeton's Cookery Book* in 1890, and went into many more editions.
14. Lady Troubridge, *Etiquette and Entertaining* (*c.* 1939), p. 91.
15. F. Marian McNeill, *The Scots Kitchen: its Lore and Recipes*, 2nd edn (1963), pp. 73–4.
16. E.M. Wright, *The Life of Joseph Wright* (1932), Vol. 2, pp. 587–93.

17. P. Brears, *Traditional Food in Yorkshire* (1987), p. 107.
18. Brontë, p. 305.
19. G.C. Warren, *The Foods We Eat* (1958), p. 116.

Chapter Five

1. For general background, see P. Brears, 'Tudor Britain', and 'Seventeenth-century Britain', in *A Taste of History*, by P. Brears and others (1993); and C.A. Wilson, 'Ideal Meals and their Menus from the Middle Ages to the Georgian Era', and P. Brears, 'Decorating the Tudor and Stuart Table', in *The Appetite and the Eye*, ed. C.A. Wilson (1991), pp. 98–121 and 56–97.
2. A. Palmer, *Movable Feasts* (1952), p. 8.
3. J. Trusler, *Honours of the Table* (1788), p. 3.
4. M. Holland, *Phaidon Guide to Silver* (1978), pp. 111–42.
5. Palmer, p. 12.
6. The extracts here regarding service at the table are all taken from Trusler, pp. 5–10.
7. The details of the early nineteenth-century dinner, which continued into Victorian times, are taken from T. Cosnett, *The Footman's Directory*, 2nd edn (1823), pp. 79–139.
8. *Hints for the Table* (1838), p. 22.
9. Ibid., p. 23.
10. See, for example, Dods, 4th edn (1829), p. 56.
11. W. Kitchiner, *The Cook's Oracle*, 4th edn (1822), pp. 45–6.
12. Dods, p. 41.
13. Kitchiner, *Cook's Oracle*, p. 53.
14. Dods, p. 52.
15. Reproduced in full colour in C. Davidson, *The World of Mary Ellen Best* (1985), p. 107.
16. *Hints for the Table*, p. 29.
17. Kitchiner, *Cook's Oracle*, p. 50.
18. Ibid. and Dods, p. 53.
19. Beeton, *Household Management* (1861), p. 964.
20. Ibid., pp. 954–5 and 911.
21. Brears, *Traditional . . . Yorkshire*, pp. 22, 28–9, 10 and 37, and note 22.
22. John Russell, *Boke of Nurture*, in *The Babees Book . . . The*

Bokes of Nurture, ed. F.J. Furnivall (Early English Text Society, OS 32, 1868), p. 137.

Chapter Six

1. A.L. Kirwan, *Host and Guest* (1864), pp. 92–3.
2. Ibid., p. 92.
3. 'The G.C.', *Round the Table* (1872), p. 12.
4. M. Bradley, *The British Housewife* (1760), p. 210.
5. 'A German Prince' (Puckler Muskau), *Tour in England, Ireland and France in the Yeaers 1826, 1827, 1828 and 1829* (English edn, 1832; new edn, 1940), Letter 4, p. 35.
6. T. Cosnett, *The Footman's Directory*, new edn (1825), p. 106.
7. F. Marin, *Les Dons de Comus* (1739), pp. 214–16.
8. G. MacDonogh, *A Palate in Revolution* (1987), p. 63.
9. Ibid., p. 69.
10. C. Pierce, *The Household Manager* (1857), p. 328.
11. *An Account of the Visit of H.R.H. the Prince Regent with their Imperial and Royal Majesties the Emperor of all the Russias and the King of Prussia to the Corporation of the City of London in June 1814*, p. 77.
12. Ibid., p. 53.
13. A. Hayward, *The Art of Dining* (1852), p. 113.
14. F.U. Dubois and E. Bernard, *La Cuisine Classique* (1856), pp. vii–xi.
15. F.U. Dubois, *Artistic Cookery* (1870), p. xiii.
16. Beeton, *Household Management* (1861), p. 955.
17. The extracts quoted in this section are all from Pierce, pp. 149–53.
18. *Etiquette for Ladies* (1894), p. 54.
19. W. Blanchard Jerrold (pseudonym: Fin Bec), *The Epicure's Year Book* (1865), p. 44.
20. *Etiquette for Ladies*, p. 60.
21. Marion Sambourne in her unpublished notebook and diaries. In this chapter the years 1880–3 are the source.
22. *Etiquette for Ladies*, p. 60. The extracts quoted through the remainder of this section are from *Etiquette for Ladies*, pp. 60–3.

23. *How to Dine* (1879), p. 44.
24. Ibid., pp. 44–5.
25. *The Ladies' Guide* (1861), pp. 63–4.
26. *Cre-fydd's Family Fare* (1866), p. cliv.
27. *How to Dine*, p. 47.
28. J.H. Walsh, *A Manual of Domestic Economy, suited to Families spending from £150 to £1500 a Year* (1890), p. 250.
29. *How to Dine*, pp. 47–8.
30. Ibid., p. 49.
31. Sambourne, diary as date, and notebook, p. 157.
32. Marshall's School of Cookery, *Specimens of Daily Bills of Fare, being Those Given during June 1890*, page for 6 June.
33. 'C.V.', *Dinners and Dinner Parties* (1862), p. 47.
34. C.H. Senn, *Dictionary of Foods and Culinary Encyclopaedia*, 5th edn (*c.* 1925), p. 147. The first edn was published *c.* 1898.
35. F.U. Dubois, *Cosmopolitan Cookery* (1868), p. xii.
36. Soyer, p. 393.

Chapter Seven

1. *Collection of Ordinances and Regulations* (1790), p. 89.
2. *Two Fifteenth-century Cookery Books*, ed. T. Austin (Early English Text Society, OS 91, 1888), p. 59; R. Warner, *Antiquitates Culinariae* (1790), p. 108.
3. T. Wright, *A History of Domestic Manners and Sentiments* (1862), p. 395.
4. Boorde, p. 252.
5. M.E. Rundell, *A New System of Domestic Cookery*, 2nd edn (1807), p. 322.
6. Beeton (1861), p. 959.
7. *Cassell's Dictionary of Cookery*, p. 944.
8. Kitchiner, *Art of Invigorating* (1822), p. 24.
9. R.K. Philp, *The Dictionary of Daily Wants* (1858), Vol. 3, p. 965.
10. Soyer, p. 400.
11. Rundell (1807), pp. 322–3.
12. Beeton (1861), p. 956.

13. *Cassell's Dictionary of Cookery*, p. 944.
14. Major L. . ., p. 55.
15. E. Copley, *The Cook's Complete Guide* (*c.* 1830), p. 730.
16. Beeton (1861), p. 956.
17. Ibid.
18. Anne Cobbett, *The English Housekeeper*, 6th edn (1851), pp. 484–5.
19. C. Dickens, *Pickwick Papers*, ed. J. Kinsley (1981), pp. 484–5. See also his *David Copperfield*, Chapter 24, where Copperfield obtains from the pastrycook's shop a pair of hot roast fowls, a dish of stewed beef with vegetables, a tart, and a shape of jelly.
20. Burnett, pp. 117–30.
21. P. Brears, 'Bastille Soup and Skilly', in *Food for the Community*, ed. C.A. Wilson (1993), pp. 135, 141, 144.
22. Beeton, new edn (*c.* 1888), p. 1441.

FURTHER READING

Beeton, I., *The Book of Household Management*. 1861. Facsimile editions, London, 1968, and later.

Brears, P., *Traditional Food in Yorkshire*. Wakefield, 1987.

Burnett, J., *Plenty and Want: a Social History of Diet in England from 1815 to the Present Day*. London, 1966.

Cobbett, A., *The English Housekeeper*. 6th edn, 1851. Facsimile edition, Wakefield, 1973.

Davidoff, L. and Hall, C., *Family Fortunes: Men and Women of the English Middle Class*. London, 1987.

Drummond, J.C. and Wilbraham, A., *The Englishman's Food*. Revised by D. Hollingworth, London, 1957. Part 4 covers the nineteenth century.

Freeman, S., *Mutton and Oysters: the Victorians and their Food*. London, 1989.

Harris, C., *The Family and Industrial Society*. London, 1983.

Horn, P., *The Rise and Fall of the Victorian Servant*. Dublin, 1975.

Lewis, J., ed., *Labour and Love: Women's Experience of Home and Family, 1850–1940*. Oxford, 1986.

Page, E.B. and Kingsford, P.W., *The Master Chefs: a History of Haute Cuisine*. London, 1971.

Palmer, A., *Movable Feasts*. London, Oxford University Press, 1952.

Rowntree, B. Seebohm, *Poverty: A Study of Town Life*. York, 1901 and later editions.

White, F., *Good Things in England*. New issue with revised index, London, 1962, and later reprints.

INDEX

Note: numbers in brackets preceded by *n* are note numbers.

INDEX